Christ in You

CHRIST IN YOU

The Christ-Life and the Self-Life

A.B. SIMPSON

CHRISTIAN PUBLICATIONS, INC
CAMP HILL, PENNSYLVANIA

Christian Publications
3825 Hartzdale Drive, Camp Hill, PA 17011

Faithful, biblical publishing since 1883

ISBN: 0-87509-635-2
© 1997 by Christian Publications
All rights reserved
Printed in the United States of America

97 98 99 00 01   5 4 3 2 1

Formerly published in two volumes
under the titles
The Christ Life
and
The Self-Life and the Christ-Life

CONTENTS

INTRODUCTION

In the late nineteenth century A.B. Simpson, the founder of The Christian and Missionary Alliance, wrote two small books on the fullness of Christ as the answer to the Christian's struggle with the self-life. For over a century these two books have ministered to those seeking a deeper walk with God. *The Christ Life* and *The Christ Life and the Self-Life*, classics in their own right, have been republished in this single volume entitled *Christ in You*.

Though written over a century ago this book is as up-to-date on the subtleties of the self-life as anything written today. Simpson is upbeat in the way he treats this subject. While being brutally realistic about man's self-centeredness he offers a message of hope in Christ. With great simplicity he expounds the profound passages in John's gospel that reveal the divine intention for Christ to indwell the Christian. Christ in us provides through His own resurrection-life full victory over the power of the sin-controlled self-life. Simpson's view of Christ's indwelling is instructional, inspirational, devotional, theological and practical.

Applied sanctification can only be a reality

when the Christian, by faith, is conscious of his union with the Lord Jesus Christ.

May God use this volume to help you learn the secret of His indwelling Presence, which truly is "the hope of glory."

CHAPTER 1

Christle the Life

The life appeared; we have seen it and testify to it, and we proclaim to you the eternal life, which was with the Father and has appeared to us.
(1 John 1:2)
He is the true God and eternal life.
(1 John 5:20)

This significant word "LIFE" is the keynote of the two profoundest books in the New Testament, the Gospel of John and the First Epistle of John. The other New Testament books tell of truth, character and righteousness but these tell us of life. The others tell the believer what to do and be, but John tells the believer the secret of becoming and accomplishing the things set before him. The mystery of nature is life. The one thing short of which all man's wisdom and resources reach is life. Science can give us the principles of things and can even reconstruct the forces of nature, but only God can give this strange and subtle thrill which sets all in spontaneous motion and gives it life.

The Sermon on the Mount tells what an ideal life should be but the Gospel of John tells how that ideal may become a reality. It starts with the mysterious secret of the new birth, where life begins, and it leads up to the highest developments of the sanctified and glorified life in the ages to come. The First Epistle of John still more fully unfolds the source, the evolution and the outflow of divine life.

Before a planet rolled, an insect hummed or an angel sang, Christ was Himself the eternal life. In the original First John 1:2 is given a stronger emphasis than the Authorized Version expresses and it reads literally thus: "We show unto you that life, the eternal, which was with the Father and was manifested unto us." First John 5:20 more fully expresses this thought, "He is the true God, and the life eternal." Jesus is the Life and from Him all life has come. The life of nature is the outflow of His creating power. The life of mind and thought and intellect is but a radiation from His infinite mind. The power that moves the universe from the mightiest sphere to the minutest spray is His personal life, for "By him all things consist" (Colossians 1:17), and "in him we live and move and have our being" (Acts 17:28). The tint of the Easter lily, the fragrance of the hyacinth, the teeming life of the vegetable world all come from Him.

Every new born soul is begotten of His life. The Church of every age and clime is the new creation of His life and power. Every saint is sustained by the life of the living Head. It is so good, therefore, to know that His life is life eternal and that in Him there is a fountain of life that never can be dry, a sufficiency that never can fail. The word "eternal" here does not merely convey the idea of existence that has neither beginning nor ending but speaks of a higher sphere of life. It is life that belongs to a loftier plane than the things that are seen and temporal. It is life that is as infinite in its scope as it is enduring in its length, a great unfathomable ocean of boundless fullness and glorious all-sufficiency.

Let us adore the Prince of Life, the Living One, the Glorious Son of God who stands before us in His radiant and eternal life proclaiming, "I am the Living One; I was dead, and behold I am alive for ever and ever. . ." (Revelation 1:18a).

The Life Manifested

"The life was manifested." This includes the whole story of the incarnation and earthly life of the Lord Jesus. This also covers the meaning of the phrase so often used by John in his Gospel and Epistle, "The Word of Life." In the original it says, "The Word of the Life." Just as a word is the expression of a human thought so He is the expression of God's thought and will, the manifestation of what was already there but unrevealed. Instead of giving man the written word alone, He sent a living Person to exhibit in the actual details of His earthly life the character of God and His purposes of love to the human race.

The story is told of a missionary who, having failed to bring conviction to the nationals in the Congo by years of preaching, at last stopped in the midst of a course of lessons on the Sermon on the Mount, and announced to the Africans that he was going to live this sermon himself among them. Before the day was over, they gave him ample opportunities of doing so by claiming all his worldly goods, and he unresistingly, gave "to him that asked, and from him that would borrow turned not away."

At nightfall the missionary's wife was in dismay, for her home was stripped, and starvation stared them in the face. But that was only the first act in the drama. Before the night was over, the Africans began to reflect upon the strange example they had witnessed. "This man," they said, "is not like the traders. He does not ask us for things, but he gives us all he has. He must be God's man, and we had better be careful how we treat him." And so the following day witnessed the scene of yesterday reversed and everything brought back with compound interest. This was the second act of the drama. The third act was a great revival, the conversion of a thousand souls and the organization of the largest church in the Congo. "The life was manifested," and they saw it, and it was an object lesson more mighty than words.

So Christ has manifested in His life the message of the Father and the meaning of the Gospel. His earthly life was a complete pattern of all that God expects a true human life to be. For the first time in the history of the race the Father beheld man of whom He could say, "In him I am well pleased."

Christ's human life covered every side of our earthly relationships that we are called to sustain. The life was manifested in every tint and shade and in every minute detail of typical human experience, so that there is no situation which can arise to which we may not apply the simple watchword. "What would Jesus do?" In our zeal for the great doctrines connected with His death, let us never depreciate the value of His life and the importance of His perfect example, both as a revelation of God and as an ideal for humanity.

The Life Crucified

While we must not undervalue the life of Christ we cannot overestimate the significance of His death.

There is a school of teachers who say much about Christian socialism and the application of Christ's example to the practical details of all our social and secular questions. But these men stop short of Calvary and leave out of view that great event which is the key of all Scripture and all Christian hope and experience. And so very soon in this deeply spiritual epistle, John introduces that expression which bids men pause with a hush of holy awe and tenderness—"The Blood."

John had hardly started his letter before two deep crimson shades had covered all the page: the one the dark stain of sin, the other the precious blood of Christ. "[T]he blood of Jesus, his Son,

purifies us from sin" (1 John 1:7). This is the great
fact back of the cross of Calvary and the resurrection. The death of Jesus Christ, the life so divine,
so human, so beautiful, laid down in sacrifice and
self-surrender, was not only as an example of sub-
mission, teaching us how to die; but a ransom for
the guilty and a satisfaction to the righteousness of
God for the sins of men.

With all his deep insight into the spirit and life
of Jesus, John, above all the disciples, recognized
the sacrificial meaning of His blood. "Behold the
Lamb of God" seems to ring out as the undertone
of his beautiful Gospel. "The blood of Jesus
Christ" is the background of his epistles. "To him
who loves us and has freed us from our sins by his
blood" is the keynote of the oft-repeated redemption song of his sublime Apocalypse. The blood of
Jesus Christ just means His life, with all its infinite value, given as a substitute and ransom for
our forfeited life.

Now it is not enough to appreciate in a sentimental way the sufferings of our Lord,
and weep in sympathy over His shame and agony. One may weep over some pathetic story of
human sorrow or under the spell of moving elo-
quence, and yet know nothing of the power of
Christ's blood. The death of Christ stands for a
great and potential fact, and is of no value until
faith enters into partnership with Him in that fact,
and knows by personal appropriation "the fellowship of his sufferings." The death of Christ simply
means for me that when He died I died, and in

God's view I am now as if I had been executed for my own sin and was now recognized as another person who has risen with Christ and is justified from his former sins because he has been executed for them, ". . . because anyone who has died has been freed from sin" (Romans 6:7). Not only so it is the secret of my sanctification, for on that cross of Calvary I, the sinful self, was put to death; and when I lay myself over with Him upon that cross and reckon myself dead, Christ's risen life passes into me and it is no longer my struggling, my goodness or my badness, but my Lord who lives in me. Therefore while I abide in Him I am counted even as He, and enabled to walk even as He walked.

Beloved, have you entered into the death of Christ and counted it yours, and through it are you now alive unto Him in the "power of His resurrection"?

The Life Risen

It is just as wrong to stop at the cross as it is to stop before the cross. It is just as wrong to have merely a dead Christ as to eliminate the death of Christ from our theology. Christ's death is only the background for His resurrection. The life that was laid down was taken up again and now He stands before us saying, "I am he that liveth, and was dead." It is not the cross with the Savior hanging on it, but it is the cross on which He hung but where He hangs no longer, the grave in which He lay but open now, and the very gateway

of life immortal. And so this passage is full of sug-
gestions of the risen Lord. ". . . and our hands
have touched—this we proclaim concerning the
Word of Life" brings to mind the morning when
He stood among them and said, "Touch me and
see; a ghost does not have flesh and bones, as you
see I have" (Luke 24:39). There is something infi-
nitely touching in language like this from the pen
of John, for he had leaned upon the Master's
breast, and doubtless he had proved the reality of
his Master's resurrection and claimed once more
the familiar place and touch of love.

And this leads us to notice that this expression—the Blood of Christ—has a higher and
deeper meaning in connection with the resurrection, for "the blood is the life" and it is the life of
Jesus Christ, His risen life as well as His atoning
death, which cleanses us from all sin. We are
"saved by His life" quite as truly as by death.

In one of the ancient types of Exodus we read of
an occasion when Moses, having sacrificed certain
bullocks at the foot of the mount and shed their
blood upon the altar, took part of the blood in ba-
sins and sprinkled it upon the people and took it
up with him into the mount where they met with
God and were accepted because of the blood. The
second action of the blood seems to denote the
resurrection life of Christ, the life taken back again
after it had been once laid down. And so with
grateful love we celebrate the victory of our risen
Lord and hail Him as the Prince of Life and the
Living One, living now as the Conqueror of death,

as the Possessor of a new life for all who are united to Him in His death and resurrection.

For this life is not for Himself but for us; having risen from the dead He now comes to relive His life in us. This is the secret of sanctification as it is unfolded in the First Epistle of John, and it is the solution of every puzzling problem in connection with that epistle. Perhaps no portion of the New Testament has so many seeming contradictions on the subject of holiness as this epistle. For example we are told in the first chapter, "If we claim to be without sin, we deceive ourselves and the truth is not in us" (1 John 1:8). And yet a little later we are told with equal emphasis, "No one who is born of God will continue to sin, because God's seed remains in him; he cannot go on sinning, because he has been born of God" (1 John 3:9). Now how can these be reconciled?

It is all very simple. First, it is true that we—that is the human "we"—have sin and have sinned. There is no good in us and we have renounced ourselves as worthless and helpless; but, on the other hand, we have taken Him to be our life and His life is a sinless one. The seed that He plants is as spotless as that beautiful bulb which, when planted in the unclean soil, grows up as pure as an angel's wing, unstained by the soil around it. It belongs to another element and is in its own nature essentially and inherently pure.

The key to this whole mystery is supplied by two verses in this epistle. "No one who lives in him keeps on sinning" (1 John 3:6). Here is the se-

cret of holiness, not our holiness but His. There is
no account made here of our perfection, but it is
only as we cling to Him and draw our life each
moment from Him that we are kept from sin. It is
the indwelling life.

Again, "We know that anyone born of God does
not continue to sin; the one who was born of God
keeps him safe, and the evil one cannot harm him"
(1 John 5:18). Here again the same truth is expressed in a different way. The only begotten Son
of God dwelling in us keeps us from the power of
sin and the assaults of Satan; and although the
devil often strikes, yet we are like the little insect
with the pane of glass between it and the bird of
prey, and "that wicked one toucheth us not."

There is one more passage which belongs to
this connection. "He who has the Son has life; he
who does not have the Son of God does not have
life" (1 John 5:12). Here it is union with the Person of the Lord Jesus that constitutes the source of
spiritual life. The secret, therefore, which Paul
had found, "Christ in you the hope of glory" (Colossians 1:27), is the secret also of the disciple who
leaned on the Master's breast. God grant that we
may know Christ, the secret of life in all His fullness, the Life Eternal, the Life Manifested, the
Life Crucified, the Resurrection Life, the Life Indwelling through Jesus Christ our Lord to whom
be glory forever and ever. Amen.

CHAPTER 2

The Personal Christ

Man remains in me, and I in him. . . apart from me you can do nothing. (John 15:5)

A missionary has stated that the Chinese have learned to differentiate between nominal Christians and true disciples. Every European resident is called a Christian, but they have learned to take those who bear this name on their merits and demerits and often have good reason to say, "If these drunken, blasphemous foreigners are Christians, then save us from Christianity." But they have found the difference between the true followers of Jesus and mere nominal Christians and they call the former not Christians but "Jesus people." They have been taught to discriminate between the outward name of Christian and true Christlikeness.

This may serve to illustrate the difference between Christian life and the Christ life. Christian life may be nothing more than the acceptance of certain ideas and principles and the observance of certain forms and rites. Christ life is a vital and divine experience through the union of the soul with the living Christ Himself. Christian life may be an honest attempt to imitate Christ and follow His teachings and commandments, but Christ-life is the incarnation of Jesus Himself in your own life. It is the Christ reliving His life in you and enabling you to be and to do what in your own strength you never could accomplish.

The first thing suggested by this thought is personality. The things we value most in the history of the past are not so much the records of events as the revelation of men and women. A country is great not through its magnificent scenery or delightful climate but because of the men and women that give it its national character. More than our traditions, memories, poetry, literature and art are our personal heroes. And in our own private life what we value most is not our houses and lands, our commerce and wealth, our culture and progress but our friends, our loved ones. You would give all the world for one frail little life that is hanging in the balance, and your dearest treasures are the persons you love and call your very own.

And so in the higher realm the greatest conception in the universe is the conception of the personal God. We rejoice to know that He is not an abstraction or principle but a living Person whom we can touch with our consciousness and embrace with the arms of our faith and love. A lady, just saved from the delusions of Christian Science, exclaimed as she apprehended the personality of Jesus Christ, "How strange that I never realized the awful error they taught me, that Christ was only a principle and not a person. I might as well try to love the grapevine on my trellis as the divine principle. Oh, I am so glad that Jesus is as real as I myself, my own blessed Savior."

The Personal Christ

As we read the story of His life, back of all His wonderful works and words is the Living One Himself, and so lofty is His personality that even infidelity has been compelled to say that the hardest thing to explain away is not the Bible but the Christ of the Bible. What other man ever talked so much of Himself or so often used the personal pronoun and yet it all seems so natural, so becoming, so majestic and so consistent with His character and personality that we listen with awe and admiration as we hear Him say, "I am the Bread of Life," "I am the Light of the world," "I and my Father are one," "Without me you can do nothing."

We instinctively feel that He has a right to stand without egotism, always in the front of the stage, and that He Himself is greater than all the truths He revealed and all the works He accomplished. And not only so, that personality is still a living Presence. "Lo, I am with you all the days." "Behold, I am alive for evermore." He walks through all the generations as really as in the days of Galilee. He is the Heart as well as the Head of Christianity, "the same yesterday and today and forever" (Hebrews 13:8).

The healing of His seamless dress
    Is by our beds of pain;
We touch Him in life's throng and press,
    And we are whole again.

But warm, sweet, tender, even yet,
    A present help is He,
And faith has still its Olivet,
    And love its Galilee.

Salvation through Personal Union with Christ

The personality of Christ is intimately connected with our salvation. We are not saved by embracing a creed or believing a doctrine but by accepting a Person. "He who has the Son has life; he who does not have the Son of God does not have life" (1 John 5:12). "Therefore, there is now no condemnation for those who are in Christ Jesus . . ." (Romans 8:1). Our relation to the Lord Jesus Himself settles our destiny. Jesus Christ is Himself the Father's Gift to sinful men, and the acceptance of that Gift brings us into fellowship with God and makes us partakers of all the benefits of redemption. Just as Adam was the living personal head of our fallen race, so Christ is the Living Head of the redeemed race and "For as in Adam all die, so in Christ all will be made alive" (1 Corinthians 15:22).

Christ Our Life

So also our deeper life is through union with

the personal Christ. The apostle has expressed this in the sublime paradox, "I have been crucified with Christ and I no longer live, but Christ lives in me. The life I live in the body I live by faith in the Son of God, who loved me and gave himself for me" (Galatians 2:20). Holiness is not personal character slowly attained but union with the Lord Jesus, so perfect and intimate that He Himself has described it under the figure of the vine and the branches and adds: "If a man remains in me and I in him, he will bear much fruit; apart from me you can do nothing" (John 15:5b). We have not to climb by slow and painful ascent the heights of holiness but to receive the Holy One Himself to dwell within us and lift us up to all the heights of grace and glory which He Himself has attained. "It is because of Him that you are in Christ Jesus, who has become for us wisdom from God—that is, our righteousness, holiness and redemption" (1 Corinthians 1:30). Our part is not to struggle after ethical culture but to receive Him, abide in Him and have Him transfer to us day by day and step by step His own excellence, His own qualities, His own graces, "grace for grace."

Christ Our Physical Life

Our physical quickening comes from the same personal source. The apostle Paul declares that the life also of Jesus was manifested in his mortal flesh. Paul had his own natural life but it was limited and often exhausted by the strain of his excessive toils and trials. But he had a second life, "the

life also of Jesus," and that enabled him to sustain
the pressures for which his own strength was in-
sufficient. The resurrection body of our glorious
Lord is the source of physical energy for all His
trusting people, and as we abide in Him and draw
from Him His sustaining strength, we may "eat
his flesh" and "drink his blood" and so "dwell" in
Him that it shall be true of us as it was of Him,
"because I live, ye shall live also."

Christ Our Hope

The glorious doctrine of His Second Coming
would be nothing without the personal Christ
Himself. It is not the reward which He is to bring
or the crown which He is to bestow which inspires the supreme longing of His followers. But it
is the person of the Lord Jesus in that blessed
place and time when at last it shall be true, "They
shall see his face," (Revelation 22:4, KJV) and ". . .
the Lamb at the center of the throne will be their
shepherd; he will lead them to springs of living
water" (7:17). The very heart of the advent hope is
this, "I will come back and take you to be with me
that you also may be where I am" (John 14:3).

Now God has specially qualified His Son to be
the sum and substance of the believer's spiritual
life. We are told in Colossians 2:9, "For in Christ
all the fullness of the Deity lives in bodily form."
God has put in Christ everything that man can
ever need. He has just concentrated and personi-
fied in this blessed Man all His own strength, love
and help for you and me. In the Vatican at Rome

there is a beautifully painted ceiling so high up
that it is impossible to see it; the visitor strains his
eye in vain to find it. To meet this difficulty, they
have constructed a mirror, so reflecting it that all
you have to do is to walk up to a little glass, and
there the minutest touches of the fresco in the
dizzy heights above are reflected right under your
eyes. So He took His glory, and beauty and help,
and put it down on the level of human ignorances
and helplessness. He just put it all in the mirror,
Jesus Christ, and said, "Is there anything in God
you need? There it is in miniature." And then He
puts it in your hand, and says, "I have put in Jesus
all I am, and now I give Him to you, and you can
claim Him for your own."

The Ideal Man

Not only is this blessed Christ the embodiment
of God's riches, but He is the pattern and sample
of what men ought to be. One Man and only One
has lived a perfect human life. With tender pathos
God says in one of the prophets: "I looked for a
man among all their tribes, and I found none." He
looked for someone that could meet the require-
ments of human character, and found none. But at
last there came One, and He looked again, and
said with delight, "This is my beloved Son, in
whom I am well pleased." "Here is my servant,
whom I uphold, my chosen one in whom I delight" (Isaiah 42:1a). He met God's expectation
and became a pattern for all men. So there has
lived One on earth who has idealized manhood

and womanhood and childhood; the sample of a
perfect character, of a woman's heart, of a man's
manhood—a pattern for the workman at the
bench, for the preacher, for the teacher, for the
friend, for the sufferer, for the tempted one—
wherever a man may be placed, Jesus has been.

And now this blessed Man is given to you. He
says, "Accept Me; not as an example to follow afar
off but as a life to come into you and impart to
you My very nature and make it second nature to
your heart, spontaneous in your choice, victorious
in your will and interwoven with all your emo-
tional life." This is the Christ life. This is the
Christ that comes to you today and offers His personal fullness and all-sufficiency.

In Harmony with Our Nature

A thoughtful, intelligent woman who was not a
Christian but had a deep hunger for that which is
right, posed the question, "How can this be so and
we not lose our individuality? This will destroy
our personality and violate our responsibility as
individuals." I said, "Your personality is incom-
plete without Christ. Christ was made for you and
you were made for Christ, and until you meet
Him you are not complete; He needs you as you
need Him. Suppose that gas jet should say, 'If I
take this fire in, the gas will lose its individuality.'
It is only when the fire comes in that the gas ful-
fills its purpose of being. Suppose the snowflake
should say, 'What shall I do? If I drop on the
ground I shall lose my individuality.' But it falls

and is absorbed by the soil, and the snowflakes are seen by and by in the primroses and daisies. It is glorious to lose ourselves and rise again in new life in Christ."

Created for Him

It took us days behind a swift engine to cross over the barren plains of the great West. Day by day nothing was seen but sand and sagebrush growing along the track. When I asked about it I found this was the best soil in the country; where the sagebrush grows, anything will grow. Only one thing was lacking. What was it? Every once in a while we came to an oasis where the grass would be greener than elsewhere; the fruits of the trop-ics—the fig tree and the orange groves—were growing. What made the difference? As we walked around these farms we found ditches which had caught the mountain stream and irri-gated the land by covering it with water. It needed but one thing to bring it out—water.

So you may have all the possibilities but you come to nothing until you let in the water and be-come fruitful. The desert needs the water, and the water needs the desert. You need Christ, and Christ needs you. It is this union, this abiding in Him and He in you, which will bring forth much fruit, for He has said, "apart from me you can do nothing" (John 15:5).

CHAPTER 3

In Christ

I know a man in Christ. (2 Corinthians 12:2)

There are two sides from which our union with Christ is presented in the Scriptures; they are best expressed by the Greek preposition "in." It gives us two hemispheres of blessing. The first is "in Christ" and the second is "Christ in you."

They are different thoughts, but each is the complement of the other and together they constitute the Christ life of which we have been speaking.

First, then, we are represented as in Christ. What is it to be in Christ? It is to be represented by Christ, to have Him stand for us and enter into all the benefits and privileges of His standing. We are in Adam inasmuch as he is our federal head. We are in our political representatives in the same sense, as they stand for and represent us. And so Christ Jesus is for us, our Representative, and His acts in a measure become ours; He acts for us rather than for Himself.

Our Sins Are Judged

In Christ our sins have been judged. His judgment on the cross was for the sins of His people. He could say in that dark hour, "Now is the time for judgment on this world" (John 12:31a). Our sins were on Him and in Him have been put away, judicially dealt with, visited with the penalty we should have borne, the shame and suffering which we deserved. Entering into union with Him by trusting Him and taking Him for our Savior saves us from the judgment we deserved. This is the first result of being in Christ, "In him we have redemption through his blood, the forgiveness of sins, in accordance with the riches of God's grace" (Ephesians 1:7). "Therefore, there is now no condemnation for those who are in Christ Jesus" (Romans 8:1). "Whoever hears my word and believes him who sent me has eternal life and will not be condemned; he has crossed over from death to life" (John 5:24).

We Are Justified

Again, if we are in Christ we are justified through His righteousness. Not only have our sins been put away but our lack of righteousness. He has met the law which we could not obey and put His own merit and righteousness to our account, and we stand in the same place as though we had kept the law and manifested the same spirit which He manifested without a single flaw. His righteousness passes over to us.

It would be possible to justify us from our sins and leave us like the poor man just saved out of prison, a wretched, homeless tramp with nothing on which to start life.

Christ not only saves us from the penalty of the law but gives us His standing. Christ is made unto us righteousness. "God made him who had no sin to be sin for us, so that in him we might become the righteousness of God" (2 Corinthians 5:21). This is the second thing that comes to us by being in Christ: sin cancelled and failure and shortcoming made up by His all-sufficient merit. What joy it inspires!

> Jesus, Thy blood and righteousness,
> My beauty are, my glorious dress.

If we are in Christ we are accepted by the Father. Our persons are accepted; we are regarded even as He is regarded and we enter into the same place He occupies. It is not merely that the judge takes the pen and blots out our sins; not even that the banker takes the pen and writes in his book our infinite credit; but the Father throws His arms around His child and takes him into Christ's very place.

It is not a millionaire making the tramp rich but a Father taking the prodigal to His bosom and making him accepted in "the Son of his love." That is what is meant by being in Christ, sin cancelled, righteousness given and we loved even as He is loved.

Sons of God

If one is in Christ, he enters into His relationships and becomes to God what Christ is. Jesus said: "My Father, and your Father; my God, and your God." And "Yet to all who received him, to those who believed in his name, he gave the right to become children of God" (John 1:12). "Ye are all the children of God by faith in Christ Jesus" (Galatians 3:26, KJV).

Two words are used in the New Testament to describe sonship. One word means a born son. But the other word means much more. The second word for sonship is almost always applied to Christ's sonship and is rarely used of anybody else but Jesus; but it is also used to denote those who enter into union with Christ. Not only are they born the children of God but they are accepted in the same sense in which Christ is; that is, they have not only the sonship of the new birth but the place of Christ Himself. They are not only sons of God but are "firstborn sons." There is a great difference in the Oriental mind between a son and the firstborn son. The firstborn was the heir; the others came in for something, but the eldest was the heir. So we are told that "that he might be the firstborn among many brothers," and believers are called the "firstborn ones." So, beloved, we are children as an angel cannot be; we are children as Jesus is. We are come "to the church of the firstborn" (Hebrews 12:23); We are "heirs of God and co-heirs with Christ" (Romans 8:17b).

Prayer Answered

In Christ we are presented by our Great High Priest before the throne in our prayers and in our worship, and we are accepted for His sake even as He Himself is accepted. He hands over the petition in your name and puts His name on the back; your prayers go to the Father as if He were asking. He is in His very person and character your Representative. He is not there in His private capacity, and we are not seen in our individual persons but as one with Christ. And when we come thus as one with Him, we shall ask what we will and it shall be given. This is the meaning of the promise, "If you remain in me and my words remain in you, ask whatever you wish, and it will be given you" (John 15:7).

Joint Heirs

We inherit all things in Christ. We sit down with Him on the throne and all His riches are ours—all things that are to come in the ages of the future. He has linked His future with us; never again can Christ possess anything without us. Beloved, if you can say, "I am Christ's" you can add, "I have all things in Him." So Paul prays for the Ephesians that they may see what Christ is: "[F]ar above all rule and authority, power and dominion, and every title that can be given, not only in the present age but also in the one to come . . . [A]nd appointed him to be head over everything . . . which is his body, the fullness of him who fills everything in every way" (Ephesians 1:21-23). He says: "All that is mine is thine." We have begun to enter into the inheritance and the ages of eternity will not exhaust its ineffable riches.

> All that He has shall be mine,
>   All that He is I shall be;
> Robed in His glory divine
>   I shall be even as He.

CHAPTER 4

Christic in Us

I will remain in you. (John 15:4)

We pass now to the second thought, "Christ in us." We look up to heaven and see Him there surrounded by all His retinue, endued with all His infinite resources and enthroned above all power and dominion. Yes, that is all mine; but there is something better. Having seen all the riches of the throne, we may bring Him down here and have Him erect that throne in our heart and make our heart a very heaven.

Christ in Heaven

If you read the epistle to the Ephesians you will see that in the first chapter the apostle prays that their eyes may look up into heaven and see what He has. Put the glass to your eye; behold that cloud. See how He ascends; He is above the grave; He is above the fetters of the tomb; He is above the forces of death and hell; He is above the forces

of nature; He is above the ranks of angels; He is
above all the things that could harm or hurt you.
And so you follow Him with the glass of faith, far
above all principality and power and might and
dominion and every name that is named until at
last, dazed with the ineffable glory, you pause
overwhelmed.

Christ in the Heart

That is one vision. But if you read further you
will see another vision. He has prayed that we
might see Christ in heaven. But now he prays that
we "may be strengthened with might in the inner
man," for something higher and grander. "What is
it, Paul? Can there be anything grander?" Oh, yes,
there is and it is this, "so that Christ may dwell in
your hearts through faith. And I pray that you,
being rooted and established in love, may have
power, together with all the saints, to grasp how
wide and long and high and deep is the love of
Christ, and to know this love that surpasses
knowledge—that you may be filled to the measure
of all the fullness of God" (Ephesians 3:17-19).
That is the other heaven, that is the heaven
brought down and put into your heart. The first
thought is Christ up there. This is Christ descend-
ing out of heaven like the New Jerusalem and
making His dwelling in your inmost being.

Christ Formed in Us

That was Paul's cry in Galatians 4:19 for his
spiritual children in Galatia. "My dear children,

for whom I am again in the pains of childbirth until Christ is formed in you." That is his prayer for those who are already Christians. "My dear children," you are regenerated; but I am travailing in birth until there shall be something more, even the very person of Christ, born in you! That is more than your being newborn. It is Christ Himself born in the newborn soul. That precious golden casket placed in the believer's breast will open and in it will come another treasure, brighter than the golden casket: the jewel of Christ's own living presence in his heart of hearts.

"My little children, born you have been, but you want a greater One to come and dwell in you; and I travail in birth, until Christ be formed in you." This is not a character to be formed but a Person coming to live in us, becoming so one with us that the government shall be on His shoulder, and we shall sing in the empire of the heart, "For to us a child is born, to us a son is given, and the government will be on his shoulders. And he will be called Wonderful Counselor, Mighty God, Everlasting Father, Prince of Peace. Of the increase of his government and peace there will be no end" (Isaiah 9:6-7).

It is the child Christ born in the heart, so that it becomes not only a converted life but a Christ life, a divine life. It is not a Christian battling and struggling alone but a Christian taking into his bosom the Lord to fight his battles, just becoming a temple for God's indwelling; so that the Infinite One can say, "I will live with them and walk

among them, and I will be their God, and they
will be my people" (2 Corinthians 6:16b). It is not,
"They shall be my people, and I will be their
God," but it is God who is first: He will be their
God and they shall be His people.

Christ's Teachings

The truth of His indwelling is found in all
Christ's deeper teachings. He did not venture to
give it in the beginning because His disciples were
not ready. He referred to it in the sixth chapter of
John and they were offended when He said: "I am
the living bread that came down from heaven. If
anyone eats of this bread, he will live forever. This
bread is my flesh, which I will give for the life of
the world" (6:51). They said: "We cannot understand Him," "This is a hard teaching," and went
away and walked with Him no more. They
thought it transcendental and sentimental.

In the fourteenth and fifteenth chapters of John
He unfolds this truth once more. He says: "Whoever has my commands and obeys them, he is the
one who loves me. He who loves me will be loved
by my Father, and I too will love him and show
myself to him. . . . "Jesus replied, 'If anyone loves
me, he will obey my teaching. My Father will love
him, and we will come to him and make our home
with him' " (John 14:21, 23). And again, in the fifteenth chapter: "I am the vine; you are the
branches. If a man remains in me and I in him, he
will bear much fruit; apart from me you can do
nothing. . . . If you remain in me and my words

remain in you, ask whatever you wish, and it will be given you" (15:5, 7). And again He says: "But the Counselor, the Holy Spirit, whom the Father will send in my name, will teach you all things, and will remind you of everything I have said to you" (14:26). In the seventeenth chapter of John He says: "Holy Father, protect them by the power of your name—the name you gave me—so that they may be one as we are one" (17:11). And He adds: "[T]hat the love you have for me may be in them and that I myself may be in them" (17:26b).

This was the last prayer Christ ever offered for His people: "That I myself may be in them." That seventeenth chapter of John was the highest utterance of Christ in this world and these last words are most precious of all. Oh, if we want His prayer fulfilled, we must enter into the meaning of this message and never stop short of its actual experience.

The Epistles

Again and again throughout the latter epistles we find this same truth repeated. In Colossians the apostle speaks of "the mystery that has been kept hidden for ages and generations, but is now disclosed to the saints" (1:26). He seems almost afraid to state it. Like someone about to tell good news he hesitates; it is so overwhelming. That mystery hidden for ages past is now to be manifested to those who believe. This truth is like the white stone with the name upon it "known only to him who receives it" (Revelation 2:17b). Paul has

at last been permitted to give the bride this signet
ring. This is the secret: "Christ in you the hope of
glory" (1:27). Have you received it? Has it been
opened to you? It is the sapphire jewel that will
outflash the glories of the New Jerusalem.

Paul testifies in Galatians 2:20, "I have been
crucified with Christ and I no longer live, but
Christ lives in me. The life I live in the body, I
live by faith in the Son of God, who loved me and
gave himself for me." That is the way Paul ob-
tained it—by dying to his own life and taking
Christ instead.

The Lord came to the isle of Patmos and gave
John this message: "Here I am! I stand at the door
and knock. If anyone hears my voice and opens
the door, I will go in and eat with him, and he
with me" (Revelation 3:20). It was written to the
Church of Laodicea—the people that called themselves the Church of God but whose hearts were
closed; self was on the throne. "I am rich," they
said; "I have acquired wealth and do not need a
thing" (Revelation 3:17). Outside stood the pleading form of Jesus, His locks wet with the dew of
the morning. Christ Himself was knocking and
waiting and saying: "If anyone hears my voice and
opens the door, I will come and eat with him, and
he with me." Oh, is it not a pathetic picture, a
shameful picture! This message was addressed to
the last of the seven Churches, the closing representative of modern Christianity; the Church of
today. He was outside the door and the church inside, satisfied to have Him there. And He is say-

ing: "But you do not realize that you are wretched, pitiful, poor, blind and naked"; while they said, "I am rich; I have acquired wealth and do not need a thing."

Christ's Own Dependence

Christ said in the fifth chapter of John that He had no independent life of His own but was constantly dependent on His Father for every word and act. The Christ life is the very life that Christ lived on this earth. Is it not strange to hear Him say, with all His resources, "By myself I can do nothing; I judge only as I hear. . ." (5:30). Jesus, who walked this earth as our Example, never tried to be independent, but He constantly received His Father's life; drew His being from His Father and lived by Him. "Just as the living Father sent me and I live because of the Father, so the one who feeds on me will live because of me" (6:57).

So He wants you and me to live by Him. He is just repeating the life He lived when He trod the hills of Galilee: utterly dependent, an empty vessel, receiving all from above. So, now, He requires you and me to be empty vessels, receiving all from Him. "In that day"—"When the spirit of Truth is come"—will He bring something that will make you important, something that will make you so pure that you will sit down and look at your holiness? Not a bit of it. This is what happens when the Holy Spirit comes into the heart: "At that day ye shall know that I am in my Father" (14:20). You shall understand how I have been linked with

Father and dependent on Him for My very life.
And you shall learn thus to depend upon Me. "On
that day you will realize that I am in my Father,
and you are in me, and I am in you" (14:20). You
will not know that you are holy and strong; but
you will know that I am holy and strong and in
you as your purity and strength.

He represents this union by the double figure of a
glorious sunrise and a home scene. First, "I will
manifest myself" (14:21, KJV). This is a Greek
word meaning to shine forth, conveying the same
idea as Isaiah when he says: "Arise, shine, for your
light has come, and the glory of the LORD rises
upon you" (60:1). This is what Jesus means when
He says: "I will manifest myself to him." How it
suggests the closing promise of the Old Testament:
"But for you who revere my name, the sun of righteousness will rise with healing in its wings . . ."
(Malachi 4:2a).

The other figure is that of the home. "[W]e will
come to him and make our home with him" (John
14:23b). He will make our spirits His dwelling
place. The once sad and sinful heart now indwelt
by Christ shall become the palace of a king, where
the believer shall dwell under the shadow of His
presence and in the joy of His fellowship.

Christ never is so distant from us
    As even to be near,
He dwells within the yielded spirit,
    And makes our heaven here.

Chapter 5

The Self-Life

The place of Saul in Old Testament history is significant and, I believe, typical of great spiritual truths. It is conceded that Israel's redemption from Egypt foreshadowed human redemption through the cross of Calvary. It is also beyond question that the triumph of Joshua and the conquest of Canaan pointed forward to the Pentecostal baptism, the blessing of the apostolic church and the deeper rest into which the Holy Spirit brings the individual Christian.

The dark period of declension recorded in Judges and the earlier chapters of Samuel typify the dark ages of Christianity. The reformation under Samuel could be compared to our Protestant Reformation and the revival of the Church from the bondage of medieval darkness and superstition. The kingdoms of David and Solomon are representative of Christ's millennial throne.

But what was the meaning of the strange parenthesis of Saul's life? I believe it represents the counterfeit kingdom that Satan is seeking to set upon the throne of human selfishness and worldly pride—the rule of the antichrist.

But while this is the dispensational meaning of Saul's life it has a still more solemn personal application for every Christian. It is God's fearful object lesson of the power and peril of the self-life and the need of its utter crucifixion before we can enter into the true kingdom of spiritual victory and power.

"Give Us a King!"

We are the spirit of self in the motive that prompted the kingdom of Saul. Samuel recognized it for what it was—a rejection of God as the supreme King of Israel and a vainglorious desire to be independent of divine control. "[N]ow appoint a king to lead us," they said, "such as all the other nations have" (1 Samuel 8:5). No wonder Samuel was displeased. When he prayed to God, God answered, "Listen to all that the people are saying to you; it is not you they have rejected, but they have rejected me as their king" (8:7).

Samuel warned the Israelites of the burdens and the trouble a king would bring upon them: "When that day comes, you will cry out for relief from the king you have chosen, and the LORD will not answer you in that day" (8:18). But Samuel's warnings were to no avail. The people had set their hearts on having a king. "We want a king over us. Then we will be like all the other nations, with a king to lead us and to go out before us and fight our battles" (8:19-20).

This is like the spirit of the prodigal son when he told his father to give him his share of the inheritance. Independence is the root of human sin, and it develops into conformity to the world. It is the broad, self-asserting and dominant "me" that would be a god.

The first step then in the new life is surrender. Everything must be yielded to God, even the things that in themselves may be harmless. Why? For no other reason than to prove our will is wholly laid down and that God is all in all.

A Splendid Figure

We see the spirit of self in the character of Saul, in the qualifications that made him the choice and the idol of the people. Saul represented all that was strong, chivalrous, attractive and promising in human nature. He was a splendid figure to behold, a head taller than all the people—"every inch a king."

He possessed the intellectual, moral and social qualities that constitute a leader. He was brave, heroic, enthusiastic and generous, and the early years of his reign are adorned with stirring examples of heroic deeds. He was all that the human heart would choose. He represented the best possibilities of human nature.

But God had to let Saul stand before the ages to show that man at his best is only man and that human self-sufficiency must end in failure and sorrow. This is the lesson that God is still trying to teach His children. Those who have learned it can

say, "I recognize that in myself." The sentence of
death has been passed on the flesh and there is
only one thing that we can do with it—nail it to
the cross of Jesus Christ, reckon it dead and keep
it forever in His bottomless grave.

All the Right Qualities

The spirit of self in Saul was combined with
much that was good and attractive both naturally
and spiritually. Naturally, we have seen that he was
not only a man of princely bearing but one of many
noble and heroic qualities. He also had a fine family.
His son Jonathan is one of the most attractive fig-
ures in the long gallery of Bible characters.

When Saul came to Samuel and was first called
to be king he seemed to have all the right qualities.
Like a dutiful son he went to search for his father's donkeys, and then he went to the prophet
Samuel to ask counsel about finding them. When
he came to Samuel and was told the extraordinary
message and anointed to be king, there was no un-
becoming self-consciousness about him. He kept
his secret with discretion and modesty.

When he left Samuel he did just what he was
told to do. When he met the company of prophets
he joined them and received a baptism of the
Spirit and prophesied among them with genuine
religious enthusiasm. And even when Samuel told
his relatives to bring him forward so that he could
present Saul to the people, Saul was hiding among
the baggage. He seemed a paragon of modesty and
unobtrusiveness.

But as we well know, Saul let the dark shadow of self blight his life and ruin his kingdom and his family. How self-deceptive is the human spirit! Later, speaking of Saul's earlier life, Samuel says, "Although you were once small in your own eyes, did you not become the head of the tribes of Israel? The LORD anointed you king over Israel" (1 Samuel 15:17).

We cannot doubt that Samuel was sincere in giving Saul credit for a measure of genuine humility. What then was the defect? It is one thing to be little in our own eyes but it is quite another thing to be out of our own sight altogether. True humility is not thinking little of ourselves; it is not thinking of ourselves at all. What we need is not so much self-denial but self-crucifixion and complete self-forgetfulness. The true spirit of Christ in us recognizes ourselves as no longer ourselves, but so completely one with the Lord Jesus that we may truly say: "I no longer live, but Christ lives in me" (Galatians 2:20).

But what are we to learn from Saul's paradoxical life? That Satan's cleverest ploy is to mix the good with the bad—to cover his poison as a sugar-coated pill. He knows we would never accept it in its uncovered form. Satan's choicest agents are those who are attractive and naturally lovely. Esau was more appealing than Jacob, but Jacob was the chosen one.

A person can be beautiful, wise, cultured, moral, useful, noble and generous but living for him or herself, and in the end be self-destroyed like Saul. Satan does not want our souls outright;

he only wants a mortgage on them. He is content
to take a lien for $1,000 if he cannot get one for
$100,000. He can wait for the day of foreclosure.
All he wants is to have his hand in it.

But God says,

"Therefore come out from them
    and be separate.
        says the Lord.

Touch no unclean thing.
    and I will receive you."
"I will be a Father to you,
    and you will be my sons and daughters,
        says the Lord Almighty."
        (2 Corinthians 6:17-18)

Saul's First Test

The first test came to Saul in an hour of severe
trial when, beleaguered by his enemies and de-
serted by almost all his soldiers, he seemed to be
facing destruction. He had been commanded by
Samuel to wait until he came to offer the burnt offering before going into battle. Seven days went
by and still no Samuel. Saul saw his men scattering and became anxious. He decided to offer up
the burnt offerings himself. But just as he was finishing up, Samuel appeared.

"What have you done?" asked Samuel.
Saul replied, "When I saw that the men

were scattering, and that you did not come
at the set time, and that the Philistines were
assembling at Micmash, . . . I felt compelled
to offer the burnt offering."

"You acted foolishly," Samuel said. "You
have not kept the command the LORD your
God gave you, if you had, he would have established your kingdom over Israel for all
time. But now your kingdom will not endure; the LORD has sought out a man after
his own heart and appointed him leader of
his people, because you have not kept the
LORD'S command." (1 Samuel 13:11-14)

Many of us live successful lives while things are
going well. But in the hour of trial self always
shows through. Saul was a splendid king until that
first trial and then he became discouraged, dis-
trustful, self-asserting and presumptuous, daring
to take in his own hands the things that belonged
only to God. He usurped God's throne thereby
showing his true nature. He was a man of his own
heart and not of God's heart, and because of that
God chose another man to lead Israel.

Because of Saul's actions God showed him how
little He needed his strength and wisdom—He
used Jonathan and his armor bearer and one
sword to defeat the Philistines and show how all-
sufficient God is to those who truly trust Him.
But Saul missed all this, nearly wrecking the victory God brought by his unthinking interference
(1 Samuel 13:23-14:45). After this it became ap-

parent that Saul could not be trusted with God's work and that his persistent self-will would always hinder the will of God.

Saul's crisis did not come immediately; God let the spirit of self work itself out. It was now evident that Saul's life would fail and that Samuel's prophecy was all too true.

A Second Test

God gave Saul another opportunity and a second test. He sent him on an important expedition to destroy Amalek, the race of Esau that had tried to hinder Israel in its passage through the wilderness.

There is a deep spiritual meaning back of this story: Amalek is a type of the flesh and it is an illustration of the principle represented by Saul's life. Saul's failure to destroy Amalek shows how deeply rooted the self-principle was in his own life. The man who spared Agag was the man who spared the principle of self in his heart. And the two pictures blend with an awful significance for us.

Saul successfully accomplished the invasion and returned smugly victorious. Upon seeing Samuel he said, "The LORD bless you! I have carried out the LORD's instructions" (1 Samuel 15:13). But the prophet's words of doom answered him back:

> What then is this bleating of sheep in my ears? What is this lowing of cattle that I hear? . . . Why did you not obey the LORD? Why did you pounce on the plunder and do

evil in the eyes of the LORD? (1 Samuel
15:14, 19).

Saul maintained that he did obey the Lord, saying that he saved the best of the plunder to sacrifice to God. But Samuel replied.

Does the LORD delight in burnt offerings
and
        sacrifices
    as much as in obeying the voice of the
        LORD?
To obey is better than sacrifice,
    and to heed is better than the fat of rams.
For rebellion is like the sin of divination,
    and arrogance like the evil of idolatry.
Because you have rejected the word of the
        LORD,
    he has rejected you as king.
            (1 Samuel 15:22-23)

It is doubtful if even then Saul fully realized
the nature of his sin. So subtle and self-deceiv-
ing is the spirit of self that all he seemed to feel
was the fear of being humiliated before the people. He begged the petty bauble of Samuel's
public recognition and honor, and this bit of
vainglory was the solace and the comfort of his
spirit when the sentence of death and ruin was
thundering in his ears.

One word above all others seems to characterize
Saul's folly-compromise. Saul obeyed only partly.

He did much good, but he compromised with evil.
God's commands are uncompromising, inexorable
and unqualified, and our obedience must be in-
flexible, absolute and complete. The faintest reser-
vation is really the spirit of disobedience. And the
failure to hearken to the full meaning of God indi-
cates a spirit of unwilling obedience.

Saul represents the incarnation of self-will and
as such, the enemy of God, even the rival of God
upon His throne.

The Canker of Self

Samuel's pronouncement against Saul did not
happen immediately. God allowed him to remain
on the throne. But it was Saul's kingdom not
God's. Saul accomplished much after this; he
fought a number of battles and established Israel
as a powerful kingdom.

All his remaining years were ones of self-activ-
ity and self-vindication. For nine of those years, he
pursued his rival David with ferocious hate. The
Spirit of God left him and an evil spirit possessed
him. And as the years went on, the beginning and
the end of his existence was self with all its miser-
able works and fruits.

Eaten out by the canker of self, his heart became the dwelling place for Satan. In the last des-
perate act of his life, Saul seeks out a medium to
tell him the outcome of the upcoming battle with
the Philistines. The Lord had rejected him, Samuel was dead and he had no one else to turn to.
It was his last fatal step. Self had driven God from

the throne of his heart, and the next chapter of the self-life was self-destruction.

From here Saul rushed with reckless despair into the last battle of his life. The next day the tragedy was complete—the flower of Israel's youth was lying on the slopes of Gilboa. The army of Saul was annihilated, the Philistines were victorious on every side and the kingdom Saul had built up for a quarter of a century for himself was broken to pieces and scattered to the winds. Even Saul's sons had been killed, and in the end Saul killed himself.

The scorpion self had stung others, and now, at last, it stung itself to death. The revelation of human selfishness was complete. We may well stand in awe and humbly, earnestly and fervently pray:

Oh, to be saved from myself, dear Lord,
    Oh, to be lost in Thee!
Oh, that it might be no more I.
    But Christ that lives in me.

Chapter 6

Subtleties of the Self-Life

*Then Samuel said, "Bring me Agag king
of the Amalekites."*

*Agag came to him confidently, thinking,
"Surely the bitterness of death is past."*

But Samuel said,

*"As your sword has made women childless,
so will your mother be childless among
women."*

*And Samuel put Agag to death before the LORD
at Gilgal. (1 Samuel 15:32-33)*

We have already referred to Samuel 15 as
an illustration of Saul's character. But we
can see other subtleties of the self-life in
the picture of Agag. Both Saul's and Agag's lives
reach the same lesson—offer the same warning—of
the peril of a self-centered life. But they reach it in
different ways, and the story of Agag is worthy of
our prayerful and heart-searching consideration.

Agag's Race

Agag belonged to the race of Amalek and the family of Esau, who represent through their entire genealogy the life of the flesh. From the beginning of the human race, God has drawn the line of demarcation between two races—the fleshly man and the spiritual man. Just outside the gate of Eden the division began. The family of Seth called themselves by the name of the Lord, while the race of Cain went off and built their city of culture and pride and became the pioneers of worldliness and wickedness.

The separation, though, soon began to disappear, and by the time of Noah the two races had mingled and intermarried. The result was progeny so degenerate and depraved that God turned with loathing from the whole race and pronounced the awful sentence, "I will wipe mankind, whom I have created, from the face of the earth" (Genesis 6:7).

After the flood God chose a separate family, the line of Abraham, and again endeavored to keep His chosen people separate. Down that family tree we see off-shoots separating from the central trunk and going out into the world. The first of these was Ishmael, a type of the spirit of bondage and sin. The next of these was Esau, the progenitor of a whole race who inherited the earthly spirit of their father—Isaac's son who sold his birthright for a morsel of meat and afterward married the daughters of Canaan, becoming as corrupt and polluted as they were. In the same line were the descendants of Lot's un-natural daughters, the Moabites and the Am-morites.

Above all this, the race of Esau and sub-sequently the Amalekites were the representatives of the spirit of the flesh and the world. This was the reason why God told Israel that they must be destroyed. We find that when the Israelites left Egypt and started on their journey to the Land of Promise, Amalek was the first to attack them. It is not difficult to see in this the foreshadowing of the fact that the first adversary we have to contend with when we leave our sinful past is the carnal nature in our own hearts. It soon asserts itself and tries to force us back into that former life. This is what Agag represents, and this is what each of us has found to be real in the experience of the Chris-tian life.

Ruler

The name of Agag is significant. It means ruler and it represents the spirit of self-will, self-asser-tion and self-dependence. It's prototype is Lucifer, the prince of light and glory, who, being lifted up with pride and refusing to be controlled, turned from an angel to a fiend and has become the des-perate leader of the rebellious hosts of hell.

We see it too in the Fall: "[Y]ou will be like God" (Genesis 3:5)—the desire for supremacy. We see it in the spirit of human ambition, in the despot, in the world conqueror, in high society and in politics. All belong to the same family—the race of Amalek and the house of Agag. Their cry is like the prodigal's "give me my share of the estate" (Luke 15:12) and let me be free from parental control to do as I please.

This spirit is found in every human heart. It may be disguised in many insidious forms and it may call itself by illustrious names and ape the highest ambitions and the noblest pretensions, but it is Agag and Satan every time. The thing in you that wants to rule and to have its own way is wrong in its nature. The first thing you need in order to be of any use anywhere is to be thoroughly broken, completely subjected and utterly crucified in the core and center of your will. Then you will accept discipline and learn to yield and obey so that God can use you as a flexible and perfectly adjusted instrument. Henceforth you will only do what God wills and choose only what God chooses.

This is the real battleground of human salvation; this is the Waterloo of every soul, this is the test question of every redeemed life. This was the point where Saul lost his kingdom and Agag lost his life and where eternal destinies are lost or won as we learn the lesson or refuse to be led in triumph by our conquering Lord.

Let us not miss the warning. Let us remember forever that no man can rule others until he himself is absolutely led of God, that no man can conquer foes until he first is conquered, that no man can lead in triumph the hosts of evil or the hearts

of men until he himself is led in triumph as the
willing captive of the Savior's love and the Master's will.

Complete Extermination

God has determined that the race of Amalek
and the house of Agag should be utterly extermi-
nated. They were not to be spared but to be destroyed. It was a case of no compromise. There
was nothing good in them.

This is God's decree against the flesh in us. It
cannot be cleansed, improved, cultivated or educated into ideals and principles. It must be exter-
minated.

What is the flesh? Is it the bad principle in
man? Is it some outward or inward evil that can
be cut away like a tumor?

> [T]he sinful mind is hostile to God. It
> does not submit to God's law, nor can it do
> so. Those controlled by the sinful nature
> cannot please God.
> You, however, are controlled not by the
> sinful nature but by the Spirit, if the Spirit
> of God lives in you. (Romans 8:7-9)

Every man who does not have the Spirit of God
is in the flesh. And everything outside the Spirit
of God is flesh. Therefore, the flesh is not simply
the sinful part of human nature but the whole of
human nature. It is the Adam race, the natural

man. It is the whole creature and the whole thing is corrupted and polluted. The tree is so crooked that it cannot be straightened without cutting it in two. The tumor is so interwoven with the flesh that you cannot cut it out without killing the man.

There is no remedy, no hope. The old life must be laid down and the new creation, wholly born of heaven and baptized with the Spirit of God, must take its place as a resurrected life, as a new creation, as an experience so supernatural and divine that its possessor can truly say, "I have been crucified with Christ and I no longer live, but Christ lives in me" (Galatians 2:20).

Do not try to sanctify the flesh or to reconstruct the kingdom of heaven out of the kingdom of hell. It is not evolution; it is creation. It is not morals or manners; it is a miracle of grace and power. Take no risks with the old man. He will fail you every time. You may think your trained hawk is a dove, but in an unsuspecting moment its beak will be buried in your flesh. Your little wolf may have all the manners of a lamb, but in an evil hour it will destroy all your lambs and perhaps rend you limb from limb.

Compromise with the Flesh

We see next in this account the attempt of man to compromise with the flesh and to disregard God's decree for complete extermination. Saul spared Agag so that he might use him to build up his triumph before the people. He kept the best of the spoil ostensibly so that he might sacrifice them to the Lord.

He obeyed God's command to a certain extent. In a sense he defeated Amelek—Saul did all God told him to do as far as it was agreeable to him. But he took his own way when it served his self-interest. His obedience therefore was not really obedience to God but obedience to self. He returned just enough of the flesh to destroy the whole service.

The essence of the disobedience was compromise, and the worst thing about it was that he tried to put the evil to good use. It was an insult in the face of heaven to bring the forbidden thing and offer it to the God he had defied. This is the spirit of modern religious culture: "Don't go too far. Don't be extreme. Don't be puritanical. Go easy. Be liberal. Meet the world halfway. Take the sinner into church because you can make good use of his money. Put that brazen-faced woman up in the choir because she will draw her theatrical set to hear her sing. Go to the theater and the play with your husband to get him to go to church with you on Sunday."

Nonsense! The devil will always get the best of you in such an unequal context, and instead of being saved the husband will drag the wife to his level. Or the operatic singer, instead of bringing her friends under the influence of religion, will bring the church to the level of her set and turn it into a clubhouse and a concert hall. The saloon keeper's money will moderate the tone of the preaching so that it will be a comfort to Sodom, and vice and sin will sit unchecked and even count

themselves the buttress and pillar of the cause of
Christ.

Do you think God will accept such service?
Will He who owns the treasures of the universe,
He who could create a mountain of gold in a moment, He who could send a thousand angels to
sing in His sanctuaries, accept the money or the
service so defiled? Will He go begging to the
devil's shrine asking his permission to let go his
captives that they may be saved? Absolutely not!
Oh, that we had the sword of Samuel to hew in
pieces the compromises that are an offense to
heaven and a disgrace to the bride of the Lamb!

Indulgence Masked in Humility

Scripture tells us that Agag, after Saul had ar-
gued with Samuel about his actions, felt confident
that he would not be killed. He came forth, walking delicately, mincing like a silly, coquettish girl,
smiling, seeking by his blandishments to disarm
opposition, to win favor—looking like an incarnation of gentleness and innocence. Indeed, he was
the perfect gentleman! Surely he could not harm a
child! Surely no one could dream of doing him
harm!

But we can recognize it for what it is—self
pleading for its life, pointing out its refinement, its
culture, its graces, the good that it is doing and
wants to do, its claim upon our consideration and
regard. It will decorate our churches with the fin-
est taste; it will sing in our choirs with all the har-
monies of classical music; it will bring society to

our churches and it will give us a bright and liberal theology. It is full of humanitarian plans for the relief of the suffering and the uplifting of degradation, and it offers us a Pullman palace car prepaid to the gates of heaven.

Surely such a beautiful, gentle creature should not be rudely slain. But despite its disguises and fawnings, the Holy Spirit divulges its true nature—the survival of self and evil.

Alive or Dead?

We see in Agag the flesh fighting death. "Surely" said Agag, "the bitterness of death is past." Similarly we find plenty of people in pulpits and pews, on platforms and in obscure corners, who would make us believe that they are dead. Yet we are reminded, when we get a good look at them, of corpses walking around in their grave clothes. They are so conscious of their deadness that we know they are alive. They are so proud of their humility that we would rather they were proud than humble. And they are so constantly in their own shadow that they try us by their religious egotism.

Surely people who are really dead do not know it, do not think about it, are unostentatious, unobtrusive, modes, simple, natural, free and, like good water, without taste, color or consciousness. Oh, for this blessed simplicity and this place of self-forgetting rest! Oh, for this fulfillment of the prayer, "Lord, let me die so dead that I will not know it!"

There is nothing so hardening to the heart as to take the place of self-surrender and then live a life of self-indulgence—calling things holy that are not, bringing the heavenly standard down to our own experience. Truly we are to reckon ourselves as dead, but we are not to reckon that we are reckoned dead. We are to reckon on a reality and to insist upon it and take nothing less from God or from ourselves. Oh, that we would dare to call things by their right names and have no counterfeit, even from ourselves!

Self Exposed

Finally, we see self exposed and slain. Agag could not deceive Samuel. The old prophet pierces him through with one glance of the Holy Spirit, and looking at his mincing, fawning figure, we can imagine him saying, "You cannot fool me. You are a murderer and a selfish, cruel tyrant. Your sword has made many a mother childless and many an innocent victim has been crushed beneath your tyranny. Behind all your smiles is a skeleton and a serpent's sting." And then with that sharp sword Samuel cut through his blandishments and hewed him to pieces before the Lord.

Sin never stops until it reaches its worst. Here God shows us the extent to which the smallest seed of selfishness can ripen.

Let us ask God to expose it in our hearts. Let us open our being to the sword of Samuel, the sword of the Holy Spirit. "For the word of God is living and active. Sharper than any double-edged sword, it penetrates even to dividing soul and spirit, joints and marrow; it judges the thoughts and attitudes of the heart" (Hebrews 4:12).

All that we need to be delivered from self and sin is to be willing to see it, to call it by its right name, to brand it with its true character, to pass sentence of death upon it, to give God the right to slay it and to stand upon the sentence without compromise. There is power enough in the sword of the Spirit, in the blood of Calvary, in the faithfulness, love and grace of God to make us dead indeed to sin but alive to God through Jesus Christ our Lord!

Chapter 7

The Shadow of Self

Now, O LORD, take away my life, for it is better for me to die than to live. (Jonah 4:3)

This was the best prayer that Jonah ever uttered—it is too bad, though, that he had the wrong intentions. The greatest need in Jonah's life was to die to Jonah. His life is an object lesson of the foolishness of the spirit of selfishness in any person, especially in anyone who professes or pretends to work for God and the souls of men.

Jonah was the first of the prophets whose writings have come down to us in the sacred canon. He lived in the reign of Jeroboam II and it was through his admonishments that Jeroboam was able to restore Israel to its former greatness.

Sent as the prophet of good tidings to his own people, Jonah gladly went. His divinely inspired messages cheered on his countrymen until they had won back the captured northern territories.

Had Jonah's career ended on this high note he would have gone into history as one of the most

successful and brilliant of Israel's prophets. But
God had other plans for Jonah. He commissioned
him to carry a message of warning to the city of
Nineveh, the mighty capital of the Assyrian em-
pire. Though the command came from God,
Jonah was reluctant to obey it. In fact, he ran—or
tried to run—in the opposite direction from
Nineveh.

Disobedience always brings separation from
God and so it was with Jonah. It was not difficult
for him to find a way out of his predicament. He
located a ship at Joppa bound for the coast of distant Tarshish and secured passage on it. But he
should have known he could not run from God.
Shortly after the ship set sail God sent a powerful
storm that nearly broke it apart. The sailors were
terrified and decided to cast lots to see who was
responsible for bringing God's wrath down upon
their ship. The lot fell on Jonah.

Realizing that the storm was his fault, Jonah
told the sailors, "Pick me up and throw me into
the sea . . . and it will become calm. I know that it
is my fault that this great storm has come upon
you" (Jonah 1:12).

At first the men were reluctant to do this;
they even tried rowing back to land. But God
was not to be put off. Finally they followed
Jonah's advice and threw him overboard. Immediately the sea calmed down and "The LORD
provided a great fish to swallow Jonah, and
Jonah was inside the fish three days and three
nights" (verse 17).

After the three days God commanded the fish to vomit up Jonah onto dry land. The word of God came to him a second time: "Go to the great city of Nineveh and proclaim to it the message I give you" (3:2). This time Jonah went without any evasion or questionings, and for a while it seemed as if he had died to self.

But it was not long before self came to the surface again. As long as his work succeeded and the people listened and repented, he was satisfied. When God in His mercy accepted the penitence of the Ninevites and cancelled His judgment upon them, Jonah was bitterly disappointed and fiercely angry. Why? Because his reputation as a prophet had supposedly been ruined. Pouting Jonah went outside the city, made a shelter from the sun and sat down under it. He was hoping God might change His mind and destroy the city. What a spectacle of humiliation and contempt! All the glory of his prophecy had been blighted by the dark shadow of self which he threw over it in his egregious folly and unspeakable selfishness.

The Test of Character

In Jonah we see a man who succeeds in the work God has given him but only as long as it is congenial. When the first test of his character comes he fails. How many of us react the same way? In the sunshine of prosperity we seem to be extraordinary workers and ideal saints. But character is more than work. God desires to see if we are truly, totally His. The tests bring us to the death of self and to the place where He can use us as His messengers.

We also see in Jonah a person who obeys and serves God as long as it suits him. In reality, though, he is a stranger to the obedience that knows no choice except the Master's will. "You are my friends if you do what I command" (John 15:14). The true friend of God does *whatever* He commands.

We see in Jonah a man destitute of the true missionary spirit, a man who thought he was full of zeal yet had no real love for God or other men. Jonah represents those people who will work hard for their own cause, even for the church, but they know nothing of the real missionary spirit. They care not for the Ninevites, the Chinese or the Africans and they think it unreasonable waste to pour out millions of dollars for the evangelization of the world. They see it better spent at home to promote the welfare of their own people.

Separation from God

When we disobey God we no longer want to be in His presence. After Adam and Eve sinned, what did they do? They hid from God. It is foolish to think we can indulge in an act of disobedience and still look upon God's face and call ourselves His children.

Jonah had no difficulty in finding a way to carry out his disobedience—Satan saw to that. The ship was ready to sail, and it was going to the right place. Jonah was soon on board and comfort-

ably asleep in his berth. The saddest thing about
backsliding is that it brings with it the devil's seda-
tives. A person can calmly sleep amid the fiercest
storm and complacently dream that all is well.
There is nothing in all the judgments of God so
terrible as a reprobate mind and a soul past feeling.

God pursued Jonah, though, and brought him
to his senses. His mercy will not let us rest in our
self-complacency and sin. Happy for us that we
have a Father who loves us so much that He is
willing to see us hurt if it drives us home to His
loving breast.

What a pity that we should compel God to
bring us back to Himself by the officers of judgment, instead of flying to the arms of His love and
choosing the blessing that He is determined we
shall not lose.

Crucifixion of the Self-Life

We see in Jonah a man who had to die to himself before he could do any real good. The great
lesson of Jonah's life is the need for crucifixion of
the self-life. In the story of Jonah we see God lov-
ingly pursuing the selfish prophet. He caused his
misfortune so that He could bless him as He really wanted to.

This was Jonah's prime opportunity to die to self.
That he did not surrender his will completely was
his own fault. He speaks of that living tomb as the
belly of Hades—the very bosom of death. The
prayer he uttered certainly sounded like the voice of

a man who meant what he said. And when he came forth it really did seem as if the old Jonah was going to be out of the picture henceforth. But as we see later, he was only half dead. God can use only a crucified person to preach about the crucified Savior.

When Jonah came out of the fish he was ready to go anywhere that God wanted him to go. When we are dead to self and sin we too will be ready to do what God commands. Our only question will be: "Lord, what will You have me do?"

Dead, but Only in Part

Despite all his suffering and humiliation we see that Jonah had only died in part. For a time he carried out God's commands. He warns the Ninevites of God's impending destruction and a great revival takes place. Everyone from the king to the lowest of his subjects is prostrate at the feet of Jehovah pleading for mercy.

But the moment God hears their cry and disappoints Jonah's predictions of their destruction, the prophet breaks down and falls into a fit of petulance and anger. God had failed to do what He had threatened, thus destroying Jonah's reputation as a prophet.

It was but another form of the self-life. A person may give up the selfishness that seeks its gratification in the pleasures of the world, yet seek gratification of the same self-life in some religious form.

The orator, for example, as he holds spellbound the hearts of thousands as he tells them about Jesus and salvation, may be just as selfish and self-

conscious as an actor on the stage or a politician on
the rostrum who speaks only for personal triumph
and ambition. Jonah's success was his snare. It led
him to forget his Master's glory and the good of
the people whom he was sent to save.

God can never use anyone until the person has
grace enough to forget him or herself entirely while
doing God's work. He will not give His glory to another or share with the most valued instrument the
praise that belongs to Jesus Christ alone.

We can never succeed in our service for God
until we learn to cast our own shadow behind us
and lose ourselves in the honor and glory of our
Master. It is said that Alexander the Great had a
famous horse that nobody could ride. Alexander
spent much time trying to break it. In the course
of his efforts he saw that the horse was afraid of its
own shadow. Leaping into the saddle one day and
turning the horse's head to the sun, he struck his
spurs into the flanks of the noble steed and dashed
off like lightning. From that moment on the fiery
charger was thoroughly subdued and it never gave
its master any trouble again. It could no longer see
its own shadow.

Oh, that we could look into the face of our Lord
and forget forever ourselves! Then He could see
us for His own glory and afford to share with us
the glory and gladness of our work.

Partakers with God

We see in Jonah a man whom God had to humble in order to save him from destroying his own

work. God loves to make us partakers with Him in the fruits of our work. We can see this in the way He honored Moses, Samuel and Paul. Their names have come down to us associated with their blessed service for the Master. But this was because they loved to forget themselves and seek only their Master's glory.

How different it was with poor Jonah! He was seeking his own glory and God had to humiliate him and let him fail in the thing he wanted. Surely "God opposes the proud/but gives grace to the humble" (James 4:6). Surely the person that would be first may well become the servant of all. As Jesus said, "If anyone would come after me, he must deny himself and take up his cross and follow me. For whoever wants to save his life will lose it, but whoever loses his life for me will find it" (Matthew 16:24). And, "Whoever serves me must follow me; and where I am, my servant also will be. My Father will honor the one who serves me" (John 12:26).

Jonah lost this honor because he sought it, and Paul found it because he renounced it and sought only to live that Jesus might be satisfied, even if Paul should be forever forgotten. This is the spirit of true service and this is the lesson that comes down to us through that humiliating spectacle sitting disappointed and rejected under the vine.

God's Great Mercy

We see in Jonah a man who wants to die when he is least prepared to die. It can only be attributed to God's great mercy that he did not take Jonah at his word and kill him when he cried with childish petulance, "Now, O LORD, take away my life, for it is better for me to die than to live" (Jonah 4:3).

Jonah asked that he might die and from the moment he disappears from the page of history and passes into an oblivion that has no ray of hope or light of recompense. The best way to be prepared to die is to be living for some high and noble purpose. The men who are ready to die are those who are needed most to live for God and their fellow men.

The True Secret of Dying

We learn one more lesson from Jonah's life: the true secret of how to die and then live for God and our own highest interest and blessing. Thank God, Jonah's life lifts our thoughts to another and a nobler life—the Lord Jesus Christ. He has died for us and taught us not only how to live with Him, but also how to die with Him. He has taught us how to live the life that has been crucified with Christ and is alive forevermore.

Not unwillingly but with His whole heart did Christ lay down His life for us, so that in His dying we might be saved from death eternal. Not for His own glory did He live and die but for us and for His Father. Only through His dying can we truly die. We can never crucify ourselves but we can be crucified with Christ and say: "I have been crucified with Christ and I no longer live, but Christ lives in me. The life I live in the body, I live by faith in the Son of God, who loved me and gave himself for me" (Galatians 2:20).

Let us learn to die, and thus let us live. Someday we shall know all the meaning of these mighty words:

> He died for me that I might die,
>   He lives for me that I might live,
> Oh, death so deep! Oh, life so high!
>   Help me to die, help me to live.

CHAPTER 8

How to Enter In

But, Lord, why do you intend to show yourself to us and not to the world? (John 14:22)

But how does He thus manifest Himself as He does not unto the world? First, He Himself brings us into this state. He does not leave us to climb up to it alone. He does not build a palace yonder and say, "If you can reach it, it will be a blessed place," but He brings us right up to the palace.

John Bunyan, when God came to him with conviction of sin, saw in vision a house of beauty and of blessing where holy men and women were singing together in the very light of the Lord. But he was outside and could not get within. It seemed that a barrier of rocks arose between them and him. He saw how happy those people were, and how bright the scene, and how real the joy. But he was out in the dark and cold. And that is the way it seems to some. They say: "It is beautiful to live a life like that where it is constant rest and victory and where our troubles do not drown

71

us; where the great whirlpool of sin does not draw us in, and we have Christ to bless us and to make us a blessing to others, but it is not possible for us to get there."

I remember a meeting where a good man got up and told the people what Christ would do for them if they would only let Him in to do it. "But," he said, "you must be prepared for it. You must get cleansed first or Christ will not come." I saw those countenances go down and the people seemed to be asking by their looks: "Oh, dear, how shall we get cleansed?" And I longed to say, "Beloved, the cleansing is just what Christ Himself waits to give you."

Christ Our Holiness

To get a holiness of our own, and then have Christ reward us for it, is not His teaching. Christ Himself is our holiness; He will bring His own holiness and come and dwell in our hearts forever.

People sometimes used to fix up the shanties on the vacant lots in the upper part of New York City where many poor people lived. The wash woman would spend a few dollars to clean up her shanty and whitewash its walls and would feel that she had made it look respectable. But when a millionaire purchased that lot, he did not fix up that old shanty, but tore it down and built a mansion in its place.

It is not fixing up the house that we need. Give Christ the vacant lot and He will excavate below the old life and build a worthier house where He

will live forever. Christ must be the preparation
for the blessing as well as the blessing. It is as
when a great Assyrian king used to set out on a
march. He did not command the people to make a
road, but he sent on his own men and they cut
down the trees and filled the broken places and
leveled the mountains. So Christ will work in us if
we let Him be the coming King and the Author
and Finisher of our faith.

Our Death to Self

A lady once told me that Christ had said to her,
"I will be thy death, and I will then be thy life."
Do not try to be your death. Take Christ for the
crucifixion. Christ will completely undertake and
finish the work of uprooting, casting away and
crucifying. One does not need to stand in the dis-
secting room working over his spiritual corpse, or
trembling with the knife of the suicide trying to
stab himself to death. Be done with all that tor-
ture. Trust Him to be the power to slay self.
Hand self over to Christ and say, "Here is the cul-
prit, Lord; I deliver him over to You. I cannot slay
him but I want him killed. I want You to still
these throbbing pulses of passion and let peace
come instead. I cannot do it. But I give You the
right to slay me in Your own way, and here once
and forevermore I yield myself to You."

Our Life and Purity

Christ will not only be the death of self and the
power to put old self aside by His Spirit and

grace, but He will be in us the new life of purity
and power. He will cleanse us and let us share His
life. And there will be such a sense of its being a
life that does not belong to you. When one receives Christ there is no pride because of one's
own goodness; but we feel like lying in the dust
and saying, "I am nothing but the chief of sin-
ners." But at the same time, He is conscious that a
blessed stream of purity is flowing through every
avenue of His being. When temptation comes He
meets it by the blessed supply of His Spirit, and
one is lifted above it; the positive destroys the
negative; the heavenly repels the earthly and the
evil.

It as when, on a sultry summer day, suddenly
the refreshing showers fall and in a few moments
everything is cleansed and purified. The grass is
fresh and green. The flowers lift up their heads
with beauty and brightness. The air is full of life
and the sweet fragrance of nature fills the senses.
So it is when the Spirit of Christ comes to refresh
the weary, sinful heart. His presence will be like
those showers, dropping upon the spirit and
cleansing it from the very dust of the defiling
earth, or like the pebble by the stream, kept clean
in its ceaseless flow.

Our Peace

Again, He is not only our death and our life but
He becomes our peace. You read much of this in the
Gospels. "My peace I give you. . . . Do not let your
hearts be troubled and do not be afraid" (John

14:27). Tranquility is one of the chief features of this life of Christ within. The natural turbulence and irritation will be stilled. One shall be self-poised or, rather, Christ-poised, and there will be a sense of calm, strength and rest. Instead of storming through life the believer will be divinely quiet. Down in the depths of life there shall be a consciousness of "And the peace of God, which transcends all understanding, will guard your hearts and your minds in Christ Jesus" (Philippians 4:7). Christ comes into the inner chambers of the heart and, although there may be turbulence and tribulation outside, whispers, "I have told you these things, so that in me you may have peace. In this world you will have trouble. But take heart! I have overcome the world" (John 16:33).

Our Joy

This indwelling Christ is more than peace—He is also joy. "That my joy may be in you and that your joy may be complete" (15:11). Zephaniah had laid hold of this thought, "The LORD your God is with you, he is mighty to save. He will take great delight in you; he will quiet you with his love, he will rejoice over you with singing" (Zephaniah 3:17). Sometimes He will be silent in His love. He will sometimes hold the tides of joy so calm and still that one will be afraid to stir for fear of breaking the spell. And then at other times the joy will sweep through all the channels of His being. Alternately He will rest and then break out in transports of joy.

The peace is abiding; the joy is occasional.
When there is need to rise above some earthly
trial, then the fountains overflow. So He came to
Paul and Silas when their bones were aching and
they were sore from the stripes of the inner
prison. They could not keep it back. They sang
for joy. It came when the people of Antioch had
chased them out of the city and "the disciples
were filled with joy and the Holy Spirit." It came
to the martyrs when they were roasting at slow
fires and they turned to their persecutors and said,
"We do not feel the flames, the joy is so great; it
fills our being and quenches the pain." It was the
Spirit of Him who, on the eve of the cross, turned
from His own troubles, began to comfort them
and said, "Do not let your hearts be troubled."

Christ in us will be our faith. We will be able to
say, "The life I live in the body, I live by the faith
of the Son of God." When you have this faith it
will be second nature to believe God. You will be
conscious of a supernatural faith, and you will not
be trying to have faith but simply responding to
His call, "Have the faith of God."

Our Love

Again the love of God will be shed abroad in
your hearts; not the love of your natural heart but
the love of God. If Christ is in you, you will be
conscious of a divine love for Christ and know
that it is not your love but His. And you will have
new affections and friendships to all men, loving
in and for Him only.

Our Wisdom

If we have this indwelling Christ, He will be our wisdom. He will in some way touch our very thoughts. He will give us new conceptions of truth. You will have His intuitions about the things you ought or ought not to do, yet all in perfect harmony with our nature, so blended with the faculties He has given us that the thoughts and impulses will seem to be our own.

Our Power

He will be the strength of God in you. Paul said, ". . .To this end I labor, struggling with all his energy, which so powerfully works in me" (Colossians 1:29). So it will not be our doing but Christ enabling us. Christ giving us His power to work for others and for the effectual building up of His kingdom. So that, while we are a weak woman or an imperfectly educated man, we will be filled with the consciousness, "I am speaking in the strength of God," and we will know that the Word of God shall not return to Him void.

He is blessed to work and speak and pray in the power of Christ. And it is mockery and worse than vain to attempt it without. Christ will be our power: "All authority in heaven and on earth has been given to me . . . " (Matthew 28:18b), ". . . surely I am with you always . . ." (Matthew 28:20b).

Our Prayer

Christ in us will be our prayer life. He will in-

tercede within us. And there will be sometimes
the groans and tears of His own Gethsemane and
again the effectual prayer that claims all things in
His name.

Our Praise

He will be our praise as well as our prayer. He
will come to the heart after it has presented its petition and touch it with the voice of thanksgiving,
enabling us to bless God for the answer that is
coming.

Our Health

If Christ is in our heart He will be our physical
strength and life. He will inspire our vital func-
tions with energy and make us know that the life
also of Jesus is being manifested in our mortal
body.

Our Patience

When Christ is in us He is our patience. One
part of Christ's life was suffering; so a large part of
ours will be suffering with Him. That cross will
also rest upon the Mount Calvary of the believer's
life and he will gladly share it with Him—not suffering needlessly, not suffering to please the enemy. It is suffering in order that a cup of cold
water might be given to another or to help carry a
burden or bear them through places where they
would sink. This is helping Christ bear His heavy
load for the suffering hearts of the world. When
suffering comes as it came to Him, from opposing

men and devils, then He will enable us to become more than conquerors.

How to Enter In

When I was in Scotland I went to visit an old cemetery in the city of Sterling and as I gazed upon one gray monument, looking back through the mist of years, it brought to my mind the story of the Covenanters. It was the monument of Margaret Wilson. It told how that dear young saint, a girl in her teens, held so to her love of Jesus that the pleadings of father and mother and friends kept her not back from death. "Only one little word, Margaret, one little word and your life will be spared," they said. "I canna speak the word that shall dishonor Jesus," she replied. "Remember your father's grief," he begged the night before she died. She stroked his gray hairs and said, "I canna speak the words you bid me speak."

Next morning they took her out—those rude, hard men—and tied her to the stake and put it in the sea. And they tied to another a gray-haired old saint, and they put her a little farther out in the wild sea so that Margaret Wilson could first see her die. And they said, "Margaret Wilson, don't you see her agony? Won't you now recant?" And she said, "No, I do not see her; I only see Jesus in His suffering servant wrestling there." And a little later the chariot of the Lord was waiting to bear her conquering spirit home.

That is our watchword, "Christ in one of His members suffering there." "Not I, but Christ."

Thus we can overcome; thus we can live; thus we can suffer. Believers can be "more than conquerors through him" (Romans 8:37).

Our Will

If Christ be thus in us He will be in the very center of our being—our will. This is the helm of character. But Christ will take the will and bend it until it shall be no longer stubborn. He will make it yield to His will and choose what He chooses. He will make it delightfully spontaneous. When I was a lad I made my own sled runners, and they would always break. But one day a carpenter showed me a better way to make runners. He put it in the steam boiler and then it would bend easily.

Christ does not want to break our will, but put it in the fire of His love and work in us to will and to do of His good pleasure. And then He will take it and make it strong. When the sled runner was bent, the carpenter showed me how to make it so firm that it would not spring back again. So Christ can make our will firm.

CHAPTER 9

How to Abide

And now, dear children, continue in him, so that when he appears we may be confident and unashamed before him at his coming. (1 John 2:28)

It would seem as though John meant that only little children could abide in Him; that only when we get to be little can we know the Lord in His fullness; only when we cease from manly or womanly strength and become dependent can we know His strength as our support and stay. John counted himself among the little children, because he says, "we" when he addresses us. He was indeed a little child in spirit from the time Boanerges died, and John laid his head on Jesus' breast to be strong no more in himself, and to be seen no more apart from the enfolding arms of Jesus.

We have seen Christ in His personal glory; we have seen what it is to be in Him and to have Him in us, and now we want to have these impressions stereotyped. John says, "Dear children, continue

in him, so that when he appears we may be confident."

How may we the believer maintain this abiding
life? You have surrendered; you have given up
your strength as well as your will; you have con-
sented that henceforth He shall support your life.
Like a true bride you have given up your very person, your name, your independence so that now
He is to be your Lord. Your very life is merged in
Him and He becomes your Head and your All in
All. Now, beloved, how is this to be maintained?
He says we are to abide, and He will abide in
some sense according to our abiding. "Abide in
me, and I in you."

Live by the Moment

First, it must be a momentary life—not a current
that flows on through its own momentum, but a
succession of little acts and habits. You have Him
for the moment and you have Him perfectly; you
are perfectly saved this moment; you are victorious
this moment, and that which fills this moment is
large enough to fill the next, so that if you shall re-
new this fellowship every moment, you shall always
abide in Him. Have you learned this? The failures
in your life mostly come through lost moments,
broken stitches, little interstices, cleavages in the
rock where the drops of water trickle down and become a torrent. But if you lose no steps and no vic-
tories you shall abide in constant triumph.

First, then, learn this secret: That you are not
sanctified for all time so that there will be no more

need for grace and victory; but you have grace for
this moment and the next moment and by the
time life is spent, you shall have had a whole
ocean of His grace. It may be a very little trickling
stream at first, but let it flow through every moment and it shall become a boundless ocean before
its course is done.

Definite Acts of Will

Next, this abiding must be established by a succession of definite acts of will and of real, fixed,
steadfast trust in Christ. It does not come as a
spontaneous and irresistible impulse that carries
you whether you will or not, but you have to begin by an act of trust and you must repeat it until
it becomes a habit. It is very important to realize
this.

A great many think when they get a blessing
that it ought to sweep them on without further effort. It is not so. An act of will, an act of choice is
the real helm of spiritual life. One is saved from
sin by actually choosing Jesus as his Savior; he is
consecrated by definitely giving up himself and
taking Christ for everything.

So, beloved, we must keep the helm fixed and
press on, moment by moment, still choosing to
trust Christ and live by Him until at last it comes
to be as natural as breathing. It is like a man res-
cued from drowning: When they take him from
the water, respiration seems to be stopped. And
when it returns, it is not spontaneous but a succession of labored pumpings; they breathe the air in

and they breathe the air out perhaps for half an hour; then an involuntary action is noticed and nature comes and makes the act spontaneous and soon the man is breathing without effort.

But it came by a definite effort at first, and by and by it became spontaneous. So with Christ: If one would have this abiding in Him become spontaneous he must make it a spiritual habit. The prophet speaks of the mind "stayed on God," and David says, "[My] heart is fixed, trusting in the LORD." (Psalm 12:7, KJV). We begin by determining, and we obey Him no matter what it costs; and by and by the habit is established.

The Law of Habit

Then comes the third principle: habit. Every habit grows out of a succession of little acts. No habit comes full-grown into your life; it grows like the roots of a tree, like the fibers of the flesh as the morsels of food are absorbed into your body. When a man goes steadily along in a course of life it is likely that that course was established by the habit of years. The stenographer takes down words as fast as they are spoken. At first it is clumsy and slow work; but at length it becomes a habit and now the stenographer does not have to stop and think how to make the characters—they come as naturally as words come to the lips. So it is with writing: We remember how painfully at first we had to hold the pen, but now dash off our signature and it is always the same; our friends know it, our banker knows it and it can be identified as ours. How did it come about? Because for years we have made the same marks. This is the reason, beloved, that it pays to plod; the habit becomes at length a necessity and is easier as it grows.

It is so with evil: it is easier for a man to go down the longer he goes down, and it is easier for him to go up the longer he goes up. And so it is with looking to Jesus: it is like the movement of the eye—the lid moves instinctively and the Bible uses it as a figure of God's care. "Keep me as the apple of thine eye." Before the dust can hurt the eye the little curtain falls over the tender eyeball. So one finds himself instinctively holding his tongue when he would have felt like talking. So he learns to discern the very scent of evil before it comes and inarticulately breathe a prayer to heaven before the danger reaches him. Thus also will the habit of obedience be formed; it comes by doing steadily, persistently and faithfully what the Lord would have us to do. He is putting us to school in these little trials, until He gets the habit confirmed, and obedience becomes easy and natural.

Self-Repression

Again, if we would abide in Christ we must continually study to have no confidence in self. Self-repression must be ever the prime necessity of divine fullness and efficiency. How quickly one springs up in self-assertion when any emergency arises. He knows how easy it was for Peter to step

forth with his sword drawn before he knew
whether he was able to meet the foe or not. That
which is done in sudden impulse can result in
weeks of regret. Take the Lord instead of impulse.
It is only as we get out of the way of the Lord that
He can use us.

And so, beloved, let us practice the repression of
self and the suspending of our will about everything until we have looked to Him and said,
"Lord, what is Your will? What is Your thought
about it?" When you have that, you and He are
not at cross-purposes; and there is blessed harmony. Those who thus abide in Christ have the
habit of reserve and quiet; they are not reckless
talkers; they will not always have an opinion
about everything, and they will not always know
what they are going to do. They will be found
holding back rash judgments, and walking softly
with God. It is the head-strong, impulsive spirit
that keeps one from hearing and following the
Lord.

Dependence

If we would abide in Christ we must remember
that Christ has undertaken not only the emergen-
cies of life, but everything; and so we must cultivate the habit of constant dependence on Him;
falling back on Him and finding Him everywhere;
recognizing that He has undertaken the business
of our life, and there is not a difficulty that comes
up, but He will carry us through if we let Him
have His way, and just trust Him.

Recognizing His Presence

Again, if you would abide in Christ you must
cultivate the habit of always recognizing Him as
near, in your heart of hearts, so that you need not
try to find Him, reaching out to the distant heav-
ens and wondering where He has gone. He is
right here; His throne is in your heart; His resources are at hand. There may be no sense of
God's presence but just accept the fact that the
Spirit is in your heart and act accordingly. Bring
everything to Him and soon the consciousness
will become real and delightful. Do not begin with
feeling—begin with acting as though He were
here. So, if you would abide in Christ, treat Him
as if He were in you and you in Him; and He will
respond to your trust and honor your confidence.

God in Everything

To abide in Christ is to recognize that Christ is
in everything that comes in life, and that everything that occurs in the course of Providence is in
some sense connected with the will of God. That
trying circumstance was not chance, something
with which Christ had nothing to do and which
we can only protest and wonder how God can let
such things be. We must believe that God led in it,
and though the floods have lifted up their heads
on high, yet God sits on the throne and is mightier
than the great sea billows and the noise of many
waters. We must believe that He will "cause the
wrath of man to praise him and the remainder

thereof will be restrain." We must say: "God is
our refuge and strength, an ever-present help in
trouble. Therefore we will not fear, though the
earth give way and the mountains fall into the
heart of the sea, though its waters roar and foam
and the mountains quake with their surging"
(Psalm 46:1-3).

Everything need not be regarded as the very
best that one would choose or the very best that
God will ultimately bring about. It is allowed
either that God may show us His power to overcome it or may teach us some lesson of holiness,
trust, tranquility or courage. It is something that,
under the circumstances, fits into God's purposes;
therefore, we are not to look for different circumstances but to conquer in these already around us.
We are not to run away and say, "I will abide in
Christ when I get to where I want to be," but we
must abide in Christ in the ship and the storm, as
well as in the harbor of blessing. Recognize that
everything is permitted by God and that He is
able to make all things work together, and not
only so, but to make us know they are all for our
good and they are working out His purposes.

Watch the Outward Senses

Abiding in Christ requires being very watch-
ful of the senses. Nothing so easily sets us wan-
dering out into dangerous fields and bypath
meadows as the senses of the body. How often
our eyes will take us away! Walking down the
street one finds a thousand things to call him

from a state of recollection. Some people's eyes are like a spider's—they see behind and before and on every side. Solomon says, "Let thine eyes look right on, and let thine eyelids look straight before thee" (Proverbs 4:25, KJV). Letting the world in, no matter by what door it comes, separates us from the presence of our Lord.

If we listen to one-hundredth part of the conversation even of Christians we will be thoroughly defiled; and so you have to hold your ears, and your eyes, and live in a little circle. One ought not to manage half so many things as he undertakes. This causes anxiety.

There is a little creature called the water spider, and it lives in the water, away down in the mud lake of the marsh. It just goes down a few inches, and lives there all the time. It has a strange apparatus by which it is able to gather around itself a bubble of air a few times larger than its body. It goes to the surface and fills it with air and goes down, and this little air bubble forms an atmosphere for it, and there it builds its nest and rears its young. Because of the principle that where the air is the water cannot enter, that spider is as safe in its little home with the dark water all around it, as it would be if it lived above in the clear air. So we can get into our element and stay there with Him, and although there is sin around us, and hell beneath us, and men are struggling and tempted and sinning, we shall be as safe as the saints above, in the heavenlies, in Christ Jesus.

Internal Prayer

Once more, if we would abide in Him, we must cultivate the habit of internal prayer, communing with God in the heart. We must know the meaning of such words as "God is spirit, and his worshipers must worship him in spirit and in truth" (John 4:24). "Give thanks in all circumstances, for this is God's will concerning you in Christ Jesus" (1 Thessalonians 5:18). This habit of silent prayer—not in words but in thought—is one of the secrets of abiding. There is an old word the mystics used—"recollection." It might be called a recollected spirit.

Vigilance

There is another word in connection with abiding: It is vigilance—being wide-awake. It is the opposite of drifting. It is the spirit of holding and being ever on guard, and yet sweetly held by the Lord. Now this does not mean that you have to do all the holding and watching; you are to have your hand on the helm and Christ will do the steering. It is like the brakes on the train—the brakeman only touches the lever and sets the current in motion; the engineer does not have to make the train go, he has only to turn the throttle. The Christian does not need to fight his battles. He has only to give the watch word, and the powers of heaven follow it up if it is in the name of Jesus. So one may ever abide in fellowship and victory moment by moment, until at last Christ becomes the atmosphere of his very life.

Let God Lead

If we would abide in Christ we must stop trying to have God help us, and fall into God's way
and let Him lead. The believer must rid himself
of the idea that he has chosen to serve Christ and
Christ must help him. Rather, he has come into
Christ's way and He is carrying him because He
cannot go any other way. If one gets on the
bosom of the river, one has to go down the river;
if one is in the bosom of God, one has to go with
Him. When the life is surrendered to God it will
be as strong as omnipotence and as sweet as
heaven.

The Unexpected

Perhaps it is well to speak of the unexpected
that may come. Sometimes the Lord lets sudden
temptations sweep over us to put us on guard.
When such things come into the life, take them as
from Him, sent to put us on the alert—like the
falling of an eyelash lets the eye know it is being
threatened. These temptations spring often from
our own heedlessness. When one is getting out of
the way the Lord permits the trial to let him know
that he had been in the enemy's country. If we
abide in Him all evil will have to strike us through
Him. Perhaps we were a little out of center and
Christ let the enemy come to frighten us back to
Him, just as the shepherd's dogs are sent to drive
the sheep into the fold. A little fall is better than
ultimately to meet with disaster.

Failures

But if, notwithstanding all his care, one makes a mistake he should not despair. He should not say, "I have lost my blessing." "I have found this life impracticable"; but remember that "If we confess our sins, he is faithful and will forgive us our sins and purify us from all unrighteousness" (1 John 1:9).

How to Make God Real

God is not real to many people. He does not seem so real to that man as his difficult task; He does not seem so real to that woman as her work and her trials; He does not seem so real to that sufferer as his sickness. How shall we make Him real? The best way I know is to take Him into the things that are real. That headache is real. Take Him into it and He will be as real as the headache, and a good deal more, for He will be there when the headache is gone. That trial is real; it has burned itself into your life; God will be more so. That washing and ironing are real; take God into your home and He will be as real. Christ is real when we link Him with our life.

So the banyan tree grows. First, its trunk and branches shoot up to heaven, and then the branches grow down into the ground and become rooted in the earth, and by and by there are a hundred branches interwoven and interlaced from the ground so that the storm and the winds cannot disturb it, and even the simoon of the Indian

Ocean cannot tear it up. It is rooted and bound together by hundreds of interlacing roots and
branches. And so when God saves a soul He
plants one branch; but when He comes to fill and
sanctify and help in your difficulties, each is another branch; and thus your life becomes rooted
and bound to God by a hundred fibers, and all the
power of hell cannot break that fellowship or separate you from His love.

Lord Jesus, make Thyself to me
A living, bright reality,
More present to faith's vision keen
Than any outward object seen,
More dear, more intimately nigh,
Than e'en the sweetest earthly tie.
Nearer and nearer still to me
Thou living, loving Saviour be.
Brighter the vision of Thy face,
More glorious still Thy words of grace;
Till life shall be transformed to love,
A heaven below, a heaven above.

CHAPTER 10

Through Death to Life

If anyone would come after me, he must deny himself and take up his cross and follow me."
(Matthew 16:24.

Here lies the great difference between the world's gospel and the Lord's gospel. The world says when it bids you goodbye, "Take care of yourself." The Lord says, "Let yourself go and take care of others and the glory of your God." The world says, "Have a good time; look out for number one." But the world gets left in the end and the last comes in first. The man that lets go gets all, and the man who holds fast loses what he has, and the Lord's words come true—"For whoever wants to save his life will lose it, but whoever loses his life for me will find it" (Matthew 16:25).

So the law of sacrifice is the greatest law in earth and heaven. The law of sacrifice is God's great law. It is written in earth and every department of nature. We tread on the skeletons of ten thousand millions of generations that have lived

and died that we might live. The very heart of the
earth itself is the wreck of ages and the buried life
of former generations.

All nature dies and lives again and each new de-
velopment is a higher and larger life built on the
wrecks of the former. A corn of wheat must fall
into the ground and die or else be a shriveled-up
seed, but as it dies it lives and multiplies and
grows into the beautiful spring, the golden
autumn and the multiplied sheaves. And so it is in
the deeper life of the higher world as you rise
from the natural to the spiritual. Everything that
is selfish is limited by ist selfishness. The river
that ceases to run becomes a stagnant pool, but as
it flows it grows fresher, richer, fuller.

If we turn our natural eye upon self we cannot
see anything. It is as we look out that the vision of
the world bursts upon us. The very law of the
natural life is love for others, caring for others by
giving away and letting go. It is death and self-destruction to be selfish.

The law of sacrifice is the law of God. God who
lived in supreme self-sufficiency as the Father,
Son and Holy Spirit gave Himself. God's glory
was in giving Himself and so He gave Himself in
the creation, in the beauty of the universe so
formed that every possible sort of happiness could
come according to its natural law. And then God
gave Himself in Jesus Christ. "God so loved the
world that he gave." He gave His best, gave His
all, gave His only begotten Son. The law of God is
sacrifice. He loved until He gave ALL.

Then it is the law of Christ Himself. He came through God's sacrifice, and He came to sacrifice. He laid His honors down, left the society of heaven for a generation, and lived with creatures farther beneath Him than the groveling earthworm is beneath man. He made Himself one of them, and became a brother of this fallen race.

He was always yielding and letting go, always holding back His power and not using it. He was always being subject to the will of the men beneath Him, until at last they nailed Him to the cross. His whole life was a continual refusing of Himself, carrying their burdens and sharing their sorrows. And so love and sacrifice is the law of Christ. "Carry each other's burdens, and in this way you will fulfill the law of Christ" (Galatians 6:2). The law of Christ is the bearing of others' burdens, the sharing of others' griefs, sacrificing yourself for another.

It is the law of Christianity. It is the law of the saint. It is the only way to be saved. From the beginning it has always been so. It was on Mount Moriah where Abraham, the father of the faithful, gave up his only child, the child of promise. It reached its climax on Mount Calvary. All alone, the way was marked by blood and sacrifice. Not only did Abraham give up his Isaac, but Isaac gave up his life and all through his life he laid himself down for others. We know how Jacob served for his wife, and then did not get the one of his choice. His was a suffering life, a passive life, a patient life.

And so Joseph died to his circumstances. Because he was to rise so high he must go down as low—down not only into banishment but into shameful imprisonment and almost into death. When Joseph was out of sight and all God's promises concerning him seemed lost and his prospects seemed hopeless, then God picked him up and set him on the world's throne.

Moses had to be a fugitive. Moses had to try and then fail, and for forty years God had to teach him and train him, and when at last Moses was out of sight He gave him his desire. At the very last moment Moses had to let go the prospect of entering the Promised Land. He died outside the gates of Canaan, sacrificed his most cherished hope and waited until the years should roll by and Jesus Himself should bring him in to stand with Him on the Mount of Transfiguration and say, "Now, Moses, you have the thing you let go, the thing you lost and died to; now you have a better resurrection." And so it was all through the past.

Saul would not give up himself, would not destroy Agag and Amalek, types of the flesh. So Saul, head and shoulders above the people, all that a man could be, went down into the darkness, sank into obscurity and shame and perhaps perdition.

There was Jonah, the man whom God honored to deliver His own people and lead His kingdom into victory and mighty power in the days of Jeroboam II, the man whom God honored to be the first foreign missionary, the man whom God picked up and sent to Assyria and said, "Go and preach to Nineveh, go bring the world to know and honor Me." God mightily blessed him. He blessed so mightily that in that city the mightiest revival the world ever saw was consummated. Yet Jonah got angry because God did not kill all the people in Nineveh and so compromised Jonah's reputation. Jonah had said that the people should die in forty days, but before the forty days were up the people repented of their sins and God repented of what He said and forgave them, and Jonah said, "Where am I in this transaction? I will never be believed again. Why did you not destroy Nineveh and save my reputation?"

And because Jonah could not let his own glory go, God had to dishonor him and leave him under the withered gourd, a sort of scarecrow to show to all generations how contemptible it is to seek one's own glory. I think there is no more shocking and ridiculous spectacle than that poor old prophet sitting under his withered gourd scolding God and begging to die just because God had dishonored him in fulfilling his mission in the repentance of the whole nation. And God just let him stand there as a spectacle of the shame and dishonor of selfishness.

The New Testament gives the story of Simon Peter's experience. The Master's last message to him when He restored him was: " 'I tell you the truth, when you were younger you dressed yourself and went where you wanted; but when you are old, you will stretch out your hands, and

someone else will dress you and lead you where
you do not want to go.' Jesus said this to indicate
the kind of death by which Peter would glorify
God." And Jesus sent him to a life of crucifixion to
be yielded, submissive, surrendered and led about
by others against his natural choice till at last he
should be crucified with downward head upon his
Master's cross.

The world says, look out for yourself; but Jesus
says, "Not I, but Christ." Not only must the old
self be crucified but the new man with all his
strength and self-confidence, too, must die. Not
only Ishmael must go out and be an outcast, but
Isaac must be yielded and not hold up his head
again.

It is so easy to talk about this. The longer I live,
the longer I know myself and friends, the more
thoroughly I am satisfied that this is the secret of
failure among Christians. Too many come a little
way with Jesus but stop at Gethsemane and Calvary. They follow Him in His ministry in Galilee.
The Sermon on the Mount was splendid morality.
They loved the feeding of the thousands, and said,
"What a blessed king He would make!" They
would not have to work as they used to. But when
He stood and talked about Calvary and the cross for
them as well as for Himself, and how they must go
with Him and go with Him all the way, they say,
"This is a hard teaching, who can bear it?"

A few days later they said, "We do not understand Him; we thought He would be a king."
They were not willing to go to the cross.

This is where multitudes have stopped short. They have said yes to self and no to God, instead of saying no to self and yes to God. It is so much easier to talk of this truth than to live it. There is no use to talk about it unless the Holy Spirit shall bring it home to us. A writer once said that there are three baptisms to be baptized with. First, the baptism of repentance when we turned from sin to God. Second, the baptism of the Holy Spirit when we receive the Holy Spirit to live in us. Third, the baptism into death after the Holy Spirit comes in. While he perhaps has no scriptural authority for this precise distinction, there is no doubt that there are these three steps to take.

After one receives the baptism of the Holy Spirit after God comes to live in him, after the Holy Spirit makes the heart His home, then it is that he has to go with Christ into His own dying and so He says, "If anyone would come after me, he must deny himself and take up his cross daily and follow me." And so He said about Himself, "I have a baptism to undergo, and how distressed I am until it is completed." I have a burial to be buried with. He was going out into deeper dying every day and His heart was all pent up with it, until He went down into Gethsemane, down into Joseph's tomb and down into Hades; and He passed through the regions of the dead and opened first the gates of heaven. That is what Jesus saw before Him after He was baptized on the banks of Jordan.

Oh, beloved, who have received the baptism of the Holy Spirit, it is you who have to go down

into His death. Now I know that in a sense we
took all that by faith when we consecrated ourselves to Christ, and we count it all real and God
counts it all real; but, my dear friends, we have to
go through it step by step. I know God treats the
believer as though it was accomplished, as though
he were sitting yonder on the throne. But he must
go through the narrow passage and the secret
places of the stairs. There must be no fooling here.
One may count it all done; but step by step it
must be written on the records of the heart.

Now, my friends, what does all this mean? It is
dying to self-will. After complete consecration to
God there often comes a tug of war. The next
morning the believer will have the most awful battle of his life. Just because he has given up his will,
the devil wants him to take it back. Do not think it
will be an Elysian field; no, it will be a battle-
field—battles with the dragon and the fiery darts.

The devil will try to show how unreasonable
consecration is, how right it is that one stand for
his own will. It will be life or death perhaps for a
week or for a month. Jesus went into the wilderness for forty days and the devil tried to have Him
have His own will, but He stood the test. He let
His own will go, "I came not to do mine own will,
but the will of him that sent me."

God could make Him a leader because He had
been led. No man can govern until he has been
governed. Joseph could not have been where he
was in Egypt unless he had been set upon by the
people, and then he sat there a broken man and a

lowly, humble spirit. His brothers came down to see him. The world would have said, "Make them feel how mean they were and how wicked." God said, "Don't be angry or grieved with yourselves; God meant it for good." If Joseph had not been humbled he would have been no good as Egypt's ruler.

No man can lead until he has been led. David had to have nine years of training, and it might have been better for him to have had nine more, then he would not have abused so shamefully his power when he got to the throne. Daniel in Babylon had to be disciplined by suffering before he could sit as Premier with Cyrus and Nebudchadnezzar. If God is going to make anything of you, let all your will go into His hands. You will find a good many tests after the first surrender but these are just opportunities for allowing the work to be done.

Then comes self-indulgence, doing a thing because we like to do it. No man has a right to do a thing for the pleasure it affords, because he enjoys or likes it. I have no right to take my dinner just because I like it. This makes me a beast. I do it because it nourishes me. Doing things just because they please us is self-seeking and wrong. "But seek first his kingdom and his righteousness." We have no divine warrant to seek ourselves in anything. Seek God and God will seek your good. Take care of the things of God because He will take care of you. Look not every man on his own things but on the things of others.

There is self-complacency, dwelling on the work
that one has done. How easy after performing some
service or gaining some victory to think, "How
good." How quickly this runs into vain glory! How
many are more interested in what people think and
say of them than what they are themselves.

In the work of God there is nothing we need to so
guard against as vanity. That was Jonah's curse.
The seraphim covered their faces with their wings,
they covered their feet with their wings. They covered their faces because they did not want to see
their beauty, and their feet because they did not
want to see their service, nor have anyone else see
them. They used only two wings to fly.

Take care how you put temptation in another's
way. It is all right to encourage workers with a
"God bless you." But don't praise. God does not
say, "How beautiful, how eloquent, how lovely,
how splendid!" That is putting on a human head
the crown that belongs to Jesus. I want the Holy
Spirit to enable me simply to do you good, but I
do not want power to bring me the honor of the
world. If I had it, I should feel it the greatest peril
of my life.

We have no more right to take Christ's honors
here than we have to sit on Jesus' throne and let
angels worship us. We have to be so careful when
God uses us to bless human souls. There is a
sweetness which is not of God. God save us from
all these snares woven by the tempter.

Philip, as soon as he had led the eunuch to Jesus, got out of the eunuch's way. Beloved, there

are subtle attachments that come between man
and man, between woman and woman, and between man and woman. They seem sweet and
right but you need much of the Holy Spirit to
keep your spirit pure. I am not talking here of sinful love. Surely it is not needful to speak of that. I
am thinking of far more subtle and refined attrac-
tions which are more dishonoring to God and
more dangerous because they are so pure. God
keep us from every service and every friendship
and every thought that is not in the Holy Spirit
and not to the honor of Jesus alone.

Then there is self-confidence that feels its
strength, spiritual or mental self-righteousness,
power to be good or do good. God has to lead us
to lay all that aside and realize our utter nothingness.

God is not pleased with the sensitiveness of the
self-life, that fine susceptibility of the feelings that
are easily wounded or that selfish desire one may
have to be loved because one seeks affection. Divine love loves that it may bless and do good. We
ought to love not because it pleases us, but because it blesses others. Paul could say, ". . . I will
very gladly spend for you everything I have and
expend myself as well. If I love you more, will
you love me less?" (2 Corinthians 12:15). He does
not say, "I will help you as long as you love me."
No; I gladly spend my last drop of blood to bless
you even when I know you don't appreciate me
the least bit. That is what is the matter with you.
People hurt you, they don't appreciate you. Well,

spend and be spent all the more when you are the less loved.

Time would fail to tell of selfish desires, covetousness, selfish motives and selfish possession, that give the believer loads of trouble, and worry, just because he insists on owning them.

There are selfish sorrows. I know of nothing more selfish than the tears we shed for our own sorrows. When God saw Israel weeping He was angry and said, "You have polluted my altar with your tears." You are weeping because you have not better bread. You are weeping because something else is dearer to you than Christ. You are weeping because you are not altogether pleased or gratified.

Our sacrifices and self-denials may be selfish. Yes, even one's claim to sanctification may be selfish. A sarcastic friend said of a person that testified about their sinlessness, "Poor old soul, she committed the biggest sin of her life for she told the biggest lie." Self can get up and pray and sit down and say, "What a lovely prayer." Self can preach a sermon and save souls and go home, pat itself on the back and say, or let the devil say through him, "You did splendidly; what a useful man you are!" Self can be burned to death and be proud of its fortitude. Yes, we can have religious selfishness as well as carnal selfishness.

How can we get rid of this? Only by seeing the danger of sin can victory be maintained. Face the sin frankly and determine that it must go. The worst of it is that it deceives us so. It says, "How that fits somebody else, not me." Many apply the truth to others and do not apply it to their own life. One must pass the sentence of death on it or else it will pass sentence on him. Sin is like the serpent with beautiful spots on it like jewels but has the sting of death in it.

May God expose everything in us that will not stand the searching flames. Let us not have a bigger gospel than we have a life. Having passed sentence of death upon self take Jesus Christ and the Holy Spirit to do the work. Don't try to fight it.

Then when the test comes and God leads us out to meet the test, let us be true. The test will often come in the very area of the self-life where the victory was won. When the battle comes, forget self; don't defend it but say, "Lord, keep me." Perhaps someone will try to provoke us. Perhaps someone will try to praise us. Just say, "Yes, the Lord let you come to see if we wanted to be appreciated." The Holy Spirit is able to take everything we dare to give and gives everything we dare to take. "To him who is able to keep you from falling and to present you without fault." What a blessed exchange it will be! Take the cross and we shall some day wear the crown, sit upon the throne, and all that He is we shall be, and all that He has we shall share.

Chapter 11

Resurrected, Not Raised

"Since, then, you have been raised with Christ" (Colossians 3:1).

There is a great difference between risen and resurrected. One may rise from one level to another; but when one is resurrected he is brought from nothingness into existence, from death to life, and the transition is simply infinite. A true Christian is not raised but resurrected.

The great objection to all the teachings of mere natural religion and human ethics is that they teach us to rise to higher planes. The glory of the gospel is that it does not teach us to rise, but shows our inability to do anything good of ourselves, and lays us at once in the grave in utter helplessness and nothingness, and then raises us up into new life, born entirely from above and sustained alone from heavenly sources.

The Christian life is not self-improving, but it is wholly supernatural and Divine. Now the resur-

rection cannot come until there has been the
death. This is presupposed, and just as real as the
death has been will be the measure of the resurrection life and power. Do not fear, therefore, to
die and to die to all that should be left behind, and
to die to self and really cease to be. We lose nothing by letting go, and we cannot enter in till we
come out. If we be dead with Him, we shall also
live with Him.

But the passage, Colossians 3:1, expresses the
fact the believer has already died and risen, and
should take the attitude of those for whom this
is an accomplished fact. He does not call upon
them here to die again with Christ and rise with
Him anew, as those who have done it are ex-
pected to live on a corresponding plane. He tells
them later in the passage, "For you died, and
your life is now hidden with Christ in God"
(Colossians 3:3).

In the sixth chapter of Romans this thought is
much more fully worked out. "All of us who were
baptized into Jesus Christ," the apostle says, "were
baptized into his death. We were therefore buried
with him through baptism into death in order
that, just as Christ was raised from the dead
through the glory of the Father, we too may live a
new life" (Romans 6:3b-4). To emphasize more
forcibly the finality of this fact he says, "For we
know that since Christ was raised from the dead,
he cannot die again; death no longer has mastery
over him. The death he died, he died to sin once
for all; but the life he lives, he lives for God."

Therefore, and in like manner, the apostle bids us to "count yourselves dead to sin but alive to God in Christ Jesus. . . . offer yourselves to God, as those who have been brought from death to life; and offer the parts of your body to him as instruments of righteousness" (Romans 6:9-11, 13).

Now much of the teaching of the day would bid us yield ourselves unto God to be crucified and to die afresh or more fully, but the apostle says nothing of the kind here. On the contrary we are to yield ourselves unto God as those who have already died and are alive from the dead, recognizing the cross as behind us; and for this very reason presenting ourselves to God to be used to His service and glory.

Have you never seen a bird soaring in midheaven with its mighty pinions spread upon the bosom of the air and floating in the clear sky without a fluttering feather or apparently the movement of a muscle? It is poised in midair; floating in the sky, far above the earth; it does not need to rise; it has risen and is benefiting from its high altitude. Very different is the movement of the little lark that springs from the ground and, beating its wings in successive efforts mounts up to the same aerial heights to sing its morning song, and then returns again to earth. One is the attitude of rising and the other is the attitude of risen.

How can we reckon ourselves dead when we find so many evidences that we are still alive, and how can we reckon ourselves risen when we find so many things that pull us back again to a lower

plane? It is the failure to reckon and abide that
drags one back. It is the recognizing of the old life
as still alive that makes it real and keeps us from
overcoming it. This is the principle which under-
lies the whole gospel system, that we receive according to the reckoning of our faith. The magic
wand of faith will lay all the ghosts that can rise in
the cemetery of the soul; and the spirit of doubt
will bring them up from the grave to haunt us as
long as we continue to question. The only way we
can ever die is by surrendering ourselves to Christ
and reckoning ourselves dead with Him.

It is a portentous fact that spiritualism claims
the power to rehabilitate in the forms of flesh and
blood the spirits of the dead. It is not an uncom-
mon thing for a deceased father to appear to his
child, and even speak to her in the old familiar
tone, and tell of things that nobody could know
but he, until the credulous mind is compelled to
believe it is the same person, and that the buried
father is truly alive. But it is not true. It is a lie. He
is as dead as when he was laid in the tomb; his
body is still there corrupting in the ground, and
his spirit is in the eternal world although he seems
to be alive. What does it mean?

It is one of the devil's lies. Satan has imperson-
ated that father. He has supernatural power to
paint upon the air the forms of those that have
passed away and to speak from those lips until
they seem to be real. This is one of the mysteries
and yet realities of the present day, and no wise or
well-informed man will attempt to dispute it. But

the explanation is this—it is simply a creation of Satan before our senses to deceive us.

What is the remedy? Refuse to recognize it. Reckon it dead. Tell it to its face it is not the father but one of the devil's brood, and it will immediately disappear. There is one thing Satan cannot stand and that is to be ignored and slighted. He lives on attention and dies of neglect. So if we will refuse to recognize the manifestation of spiritualism, we will always find that it will disappear and have no power to continue its movements. It is wholly dependent on the consent of the will.

Now here is a fine illustration of the principle of the gospel. One surrenders himself to Christ to be crucified with Him, and to have all the old life pass out, and henceforth to live as one born from heaven and animated by Him alone. Suddenly some of his old traits of evil reappear—old though—evil tendencies assert themselves and say loudly, "We are not dead." Now if he recognizes these things, fears them and obeys them, they will control him and drag him back into the former state. But if he refuses to recognize them, and says, "These are Satan's lies, I am dead indeed unto sin; these do not belong unto me, but are the children of the devil, I therefore repudiate them and rise above them," God will detach him from them and make them utterly dead. They were no part of him, but simply temptations which Satan tried to throw over him, and to weave around him that which seemed part of himself.

This is the true remedy for all the workings of

temptation and sin. It is an awful fact that when one counts himself wicked he will become wicked. Let that pure girl be but made to believe that she is degraded and lost to virtue, and she will have no heart to be pure. She will recklessly sink to all depths of sin. Let the child of God but begin to doubt his acceptance and expect to look upon his Father's face with a frown, and he will have no heart to be holy, he will sink into disobedience, discouragement and sin.

There is a strange story written by a gifted mind, describing a man who was two men alternately. When he believed himself to be a noble character, he was noble true, and lived accordingly; but when the other ideal took possession of him and made him feel degraded, he went down accordingly. "As a man thinketh in his heart, so is he." Our reckonings often reflect themselves in our realities; therefore, God has made this principle of faith to be the mainspring of personal righteousness and holiness, and the subtle, yet sublime, power that can lead men out of themselves into the very life of God.

Beloved, shall we let the Master teach us not so much to rise as to remember we are risen—that we have been raised with Christ from the dead, resurrected from the grave of our nothingness and worse than nothingness, and that we are sitting with Him in heavenly places, recognized by the Father and permitted to reckon ourselves as being "even as He"?

Our attitude will influence our aim. People live

according to their standing. The highborn child of nobility carries in his bearing and his mien the consciousness of his noble descent, and so those who have their title to be on high—and consciousness of their high and heavenly rank—walk as children of the kingdom. The remainder of this chapter is devoted to working out this most practical idea because to be risen with Christ is to live accordingly.

The argument against lying is that one must put off the old man and put on the new man. The believer has ceased to be a pauper and has become a prince. Therefore we are to put off the rags of the beggar and wear the epaulette of the prince. We have put on the new man therefore let us put on kindness, humbleness of mind, meekness, long-suffering and over all that charity, which is a perfect girdle that binds all the garments together. We are to put on Christ Himself, the best of all our robes. This resurrection life is intensely practical. The apostle brings it into touch with the closest relationships of life, with the family circle, with masters and servants, and with all the secular obligations of life. It is to affect our whole conduct and leads us to walk wherever He calls.

This draws attention to the practical power there is in being raised up together with Christ. It has power, in the first place, to confirm our hope and assurance of salvation because the resurrection of Jesus was the finishing work and a guarantee to men and angels that the ransom price was paid and the work of atonement complete.

When Jesus came forth triumphant from the
tomb, it was evident to the universe that the purpose for which He went there was fulfilled, the
work He undertook was satisfactorily done, and the
Father was satisfied with His finished atonement.
Therefore, faith can rest upon His resurrection, as
an everlasting foundation, and say: "Who is he that
condemns? Christ Jesus, who died—more than that,
who was raised to life—is at the right hand of God
and is also interceding for us" (Romans 8:34).

The resurrection of Christ is the power that
sanctifies. It enables us to count our own life, our
former self, annihilated, so that we are no longer
the same person in the eyes of God, and may with
confidence repudiate self, and refuse either to
obey or fear our former evil nature. Indeed, it is
the risen Christ Himself who comes to dwell
within, and becomes the power of this new life
and victorious obedience.

It is not merely the fact of the resurrection, but
the fellowship of the Risen One that brings victory and power. One has learned the meaning of
the sublime paradox, "I have been crucified with
Christ and I no longer live, but Christ lives in
me." This is the only true and lasting sanctification, the indwelling life of Christ, the Risen One,
in the believing and obedient soul.

There is power in the resurrection to heal us.
He that came forth from the tomb on that Easter
morning was the physical Christ, and that body of
His is the Head of our bodies, and the foundation
of physical strength, as well as spiritual life. If we

will receive and trust Him, He will do as much for our bodies as for our spirits, and we shall find a new supernatural strength as the power of the future resurrection touches our physical bodies.

Christ's resurrection also energizes faith and encourages the believer to claim answers to prayer, and ask difficult or impossible things from God. What can be too difficult or impossible after the open grave and the stone rolled away? God is trying to teach us. . . "his incomparably great power for us who believe. That power is like the working of his mighty strength, which he exerted in Christ when he raised him from the dead and seated him at his right hand in the heavenly realms" (Ephesians 1:19-20). This is the measure that God is able and willing to do in the name of Jesus under a Christian dispensation. Christ's resurrection is a pledge of all we can ask for, and if we fully believed in the power of that resurrection we would take much more than we have ever done.

The resurrection of the Lord Jesus Christ is the power for true service. The testimony of His resurrection is always peculiarly used by the Holy Spirit as the power of God unto the salvation of men. It was the chief theme of the ministry of the early apostles. They were always preaching of Jesus and the resurrection. It gives a peculiar brightness and attractiveness to Christian life and Christian work. Many Christians look as gloomy as if they were going to their own funeral. We heard not long ago of a little girl who met some gloomy-looking people on the road and she said,

"Mother, those are Christians, aren't they?" And when the mother asked her why she thought so she said, "They look so unhappy."

This is the type of Christianity that comes from the cloister and the cross. This is not the Easter type, and certainly it is not the higher type. The religion of Jesus should be as bright as the blossoms of the spring, the songs of the warbling birds and the springing pulses of reviving nature. Our Lord met the women on that bright morning with the cheering message, "All hail," and so He would meet each one that believes on the morning of his new Christian life and bid him go forth with the joy of the Lord as his strength.

This joy springs from the resurrection and is maintained in the heavenlies by the ascended Lord. This is the message that a sad and sinful world needs today. Its motto must not be the "Ecce homo" of the judgment hall, but the glad "All hail!" of the Easter dawn. The more of the indwelling Christ and the resurrection life there is in Christian work, the more will be its power to attract, sanctify and save the world.

Christ's resurrection enables us to meet the hardest places in life and endure its bitterest trials. Philippians says that the power of His resurrection is to bring us into the fellowship of His sufferings, and make us conformable unto His death. We go into the resurrection life that we may be strong enough to suffer with Him and for Him.

Now, let there be no misunderstanding here. This does not mean personal suffering through sickness or struggles of the spiritual life. These sufferings ought to belong to the earlier period of our experiences. Christ had no conflicts about His sanctification and no physical disease to contend with during His life. So, in bearing these the believer is not bearing the sufferings of Christ. His sufferings are for others, and the power of His resurrection will bring us to share His high and holy sorrows for His suffering church and a dying world. It is a fact that the harder the place and the lower the sphere of toil and suffering, the more the elevation of His grace and glory is needed to meet it. From the heights we must reach the depths.

The epistles, which lift us into heavenly places, bring us back in every instance to the most commonplace duties, the most ordinary relationships and the most severe trials. These letters to the Ephesians and the Colossians, which speak about the highest altitudes of faith and power, speak also more than any others of the temptations common to men, and the duties of husbands and wives, and the need of truthfulness, sobriety, honesty and righteousness and all the most unromantic, practical experiences of human life.

There is a very remarkable passage in Isaiah which seems to be parallel with the thought in Philippians. It tells us of those that mount up with wings as eagles; but immediately afterward we find the same persons coming down to the ordinary walks of life, to "run and not grow weary, . . . walk and not faint." It would seem as if the

mounting up was just intended to fit them for the
running and walking, and that the higher experiences of grace and glory were just designed to enable them to tread the lower level of toil and trial.
It is in keeping with this that the apostle speaks of
glorying in tribulation. "Glory" expresses the
highest attitude of the soul, and "tribulation" the
deepest degree of suffering.

It teaches that when we come to the deepest
and lowest place we must meet it in the highest
and most heavenly spirit. This is coming down
from the Mount of Transfiguration to meet the
demoniac in the plain below and cast out the
power of Satan from a suffering world. Yes, these
are the sufferings of Christ. The power of His resurrection is designed to prepare us, enable us and
help us to rise into all the heights of His glorious
life, that like Him we may go forth to reflect it in
blessing upon the lives of others, and find even
sweeter joy in the ministrations of holy love than
we have in the ecstasies of the Divine communion.

Resurrected with my risen Saviour,
    Seated with Him at His own right hand;
This the glorious message Easter brings me.
    This the place in which by faith I stand.

Men would bid you rise to higher levels.
    But they leave you on the human plane.
We must have a heavenly resurrection;
    We must die with Christ and rise again.

Once there lived another man within me,
    Child of earth and slave of Satan he;
But I nailed him to the cross of Jesus,
    And that man is nothing now to me.

Now another man is living in me,
    And I count His blessed life as mine;
I have died with Him to all my own life;
    I have risen to all His life Divine.

Oh, it is so sweet to die with Jesus!
    And by death be free from self and sin.
Oh, it is so sweet to live with Jesus!
    As He lives the death-born life within.

CHAPTER 12

Union with Christ

Both the one who makes men holy and those who are made holy are of the same family. So Jesus is not ashamed to call them brothers.
(Hebrews 2:11)

This whole passage is a beautiful picture of our identification with Christ. We are . . .

One with Him in Nature

"Since the children have flesh and blood, he too shared in their humanity . . ." (Hebrews 2:14a). "For surely it is not angels he helps, but Abraham's descendants" (Hebrews 2:16). How precious this word "shared!" He has the very same humanity with man and by actual sympathy understands every instinct, feeling, hope and fear. Not only has He a human body, but a reasonable soul and all the attributes of mind and all the sensibilities of heart which we possess, and not only so, He still retains this perfect humanity. He has carried it to the right hand of God.

Partaker of the human name,
He knows the frailty of our frame.

Let not the transcendent glory of His Deity ob-
scure this glorious important truth. He who is the
Son of God is equally the Son of Man. But next,
He is also . . .

One in Sonship

"So Jesus is not ashamed to call them brothers."
"Behold I and the children whom God hath given
me" (Hebrews 2:13, KJV). Not only does He
come down into humanity, but He also takes the
saints up into His Divinity; for they are, indeed,
through Him, "partakers of the Divine nature."
His own very being is imparted to the believer
and He shares His actual relation to the Father.
"Go instead to my brothers and tell them, 'I am
returning to my Father and your Father, to my
God and your God.'" It is not that we are
adopted into sonship, as a poor child of obscure
birth may be received into a noble family, to become the legalized son and heir, but it is as if that
child could be reborn into the very blood of that
highborn house. We have been actually made partakers of the same nature as God.

Hence the apostle John has finely expressed the
deep reality of our sonship in his wonderful
words, "Behold what manner of love the Father
hath bestowed upon us that we should be called
the sons of God" (1 John 3:1); and then he adds,
"and we are the sons of God," not merely called

and even legally declared the sons of God, but actually the sons of God by receiving the life and nature of God and therefore the brethren of our Lord—not only in His human nature but still more in His divine relationship. "So Jesus is not ashamed to call them brothers."

He gives us that which entitles us to that right and makes us worthy of it. He does not introduce us into a position for which we are uneducated and unfitted but He gives us a nature worthy of our glorious standing; and as He shall look upon us in our complete and glorious exaltation—reflecting His own likeness and shining in His Father's glory—He shall have no cause to be ashamed of us.

Even now He is pleased to acknowledge us before the universe and call us brethren in the sight of all earth and heaven. Oh, how this dignifies the humblest saint of God! How little we need mind the misunderstandings of the world if He "is not ashamed to call us brethren!"

It is said that an English officer was once being treated with neglect and scorn by his fellow officers on account of his promotion from an obscure position to higher rank. They were not willing to forget his humble birth and passed him by with neglect and coldness. His commanding officer heard of it and so one day he stepped into his tent and talked to him for some time, and then taking him by the arm, the two of them walked for half an hour in front of the other officers' tents. The officers saluted their commanding officer as he passed them, in profound respect in which his companion shared. He then left the ground while they looked after him in amazement and humiliation, and after that day there was no lack of respect for the new officer. His commander was not ashamed to own him.

Thus our blessed Brother claims kinship with the believer before earth and heaven; thus He presents his prayers before the throne and owns his name before His Father's face and makes the name of a mortal to be honored in the highest court in this universe.

One in Spiritual Experience

But again, He is one with us in spiritual experience. The same grace which we receive He also had to receive; the same faith which we have to exercise He exercised. In this passage He speaks of putting His trust in God just as we trust, and praising Him for deliverance in the midst of the church just as we do when we receive our blessings. The great Forerunner has already passed over the pathway of the Christian life, so wherever the sheep follow He has gone before.

This wonderful truth is sometimes difficult to realize. Christ is depicted as dropping down from heaven with a life all foreign and sublime, that we do not quite take in without much thought, the full meaning of His teachings that He, like us, was led through all the discipline of a life of faith and dependence: that He could truly say, "The Son can do nothing by himself; he can do only what he sees his Father doing, because whatever the Father does the Son also does" (John 5:19). "Just as the living Father sent me and I live because of the Father, so the one who feeds on me will live because of me" (John 6:57). He was dependent on the resources of prayer, communion with God, the constant supply of the Holy Spirit, and He understands all the struggles of spiritual life by actual affinity.

Hence we find Him in the prophetic picture exclaiming, "Therefore have I set my face like a flint, and I know I will not be put to shame. He who vindicates me is near. Who then will bring charges against me?" (Isaiah 50:7-8). This was the language of faith, a faith that overcame in the hour of trial, just as we overcome. Not only had He the same experience as we, but He brings us into His very experience. This is really the nature of true sanctification, that it imparts to us the sanctity of Christ. This is the meaning of the passage: "He that sanctifieth and they who are sanctified are all one." He gives His own sanctity and makes His people one with Him in His spirit of holiness. It was this that He meant when He said, "For them I sanctify myself, that they too may be truly sanctified" (John 17:19). He consecrated Himself to live in His people and reproduce His own pure and perfect life in their experience. Holiness is thus the indwelling of the Holy Christ, the unity of a human spirit with the spirit of Jesus.

But again, He is . . .

One with Us in Trial

"In bringing many sons to glory, it was fitting that God, for whom and through whom everything exists, should make the author of their salvation perfect through suffering"; "therefore he was in all points tempted like as we are, yet without sin." Therefore He has passed through every variety of human suffering and is now able, from actual experience, to sympathize with the succor those who are tempted and to make them realize that they are never alone in their afflictions, but understood by His kindred heart and sustained by His sympathy and love.

Not only so but He still retains this power of sympathy and feels the throb of our every pain, for He is able to be "touched with the feeling of our infirmities." The word "touched" expresses a great deal. It means that our troubles are His troubles and that in all our afflictions He is afflicted. It is not a sympathy of sentiment but a sympathy of suffering.

There is much help in this for the tired heart. It is the foundation of His Priesthood and God meant that it should be to us a source of unceasing consolation. Let us realize more fully our oneness with our Great High Priest and cast all our burdens on His great heart of suffering love. If we know what it is to ache in every nerve with the responsive pain of our suffering child, we can form some idea how our sorrows touch His heart and thrill His exalted frame. As the mother feels her baby's pain, as the heart of friendship echoes every cry from another's woe, so in heaven our exalted Savior—even amid the raptures of that happy world, suffers with all His children bear. "Therefore, since we have a great high priest . . . [l]et us then approach the throne of grace with confidence" (Hebrews 4:14a, 16a). Let us bear with patience the yoke as He carries the heavier end. But He is also. . .

One with us in Death

Not only does He suffer all the trials of His lot but He is not exempt from mortal fate; for we read that God appointed that He through the grace of God should taste death for every man, ". . . that by his death he might destroy him who holds the power of death—that is, the devil—and free those who all their lives were held in slavery by their fear of death" (Hebrews 2:14-15). Even the dark gates of this last prison house He too has entered. There is something very suggestive in the expression that "He should taste death for every man." It seems to suggest that he had all the bitterness of the cup to drain and has taken the taste out of death for all who are united with Him. There is no poison in the cup now and no virulence in the sting. He tasted it; but the bitterness of death is past if we are in Him. "For if a man keep my sayings he shall never see death." He shall only see the face of our blessed Lord and the open gates of heaven. All the death that was in the cup, Christ has drunk, and there is the glad shout,

"But thanks be to God! He gives us the victory through our Lord Jesus Christ" (1 Corinthains 15:57).

> Death and the curse were in the cup;
> Oh, Christ, 'twas full for Thee!
> But Thou has drained the last dark drop,
> 'Tis empty now for me.
> For me, Lord Jesus, Thou hast died,
> And I have died in Thee;
> Thou 'rt risen, my bands are all untied,
> And now Thou livest in me.

Finally, He is . . .

One with Us in Glorious Destiny

The writer of the book of Hebrews quotes from the eighth Psalm which describes the future dignity and destiny of man. The psalmist speaks of the glorious dignity of man in these words, ". . . you put everything under his feet" (Psalm 8:6b), and the apostle argues if this be literally true, it implies a dignity that leaves nothing that is not put under man, but he says as a matter of actual observation, "and put everything under his feet" (Hebrews 2:8b). How then can the words be true of man?

The glorious explanation is that they are true of the Son of Man, the Great Head of the race. "But we see Jesus . . . now crowned with glory and honor" (2:9a). He takes up the honor of the race and wins the crown of dominion for humanity, and then he shares it all with us. For all that He has won He has won as a man for redeemed humanity; and has raised us up with Him to sit in heavenly places, that in the ages to come He might show the exceeding riches of His grace in His kindness to us by Christ Jesus. Every crown He wears He shall share with us. "To him who overcomes, I will give the right to sit on my throne, just as I overcame and sat down with my Father on his throne" (Revelation 3:21). This is the high and glorious hope of every child of God. This is the meaning of our union with the Son of God. Well may the apostle say, "Dear friends, now we are children of God, and what we will be has not yet been made known. But we know that when he appears, we shall be like him, for we shall see him as he is" (1 John 3:2). Such a hope may well inspire and unspeakably encourage the children of God.

Let us think of some of its practical applications: First, let us learn the secret of even of our faith. It is the faith of Christ springing in our hearts and trusting in our trials. So shall we also sing, "The life that I now live, I live by faith in the Son of God, who loved me and gave Himself for me" (Galatians 2:20). Thus looking off unto Jesus, "The Author and Finisher of our faith," we shall lie down upon them in blessed repose and be borne up by them with the faith which is no more our own than the promises upon which it rests. Each new need will find us leaning afresh on Him for the grace to trust and to overcome.

The true spirit of prayer is the spirit of Christ in

us. "In the midst of the church will I sing praises unto thee." Christ still sings these praises in the trusting heart and lifts his prayers into songs of victory. Paul and Silas knew the true spirit of prayer in the prison of Philippi and turned prayer into praise, night into day, the sorrow into joy. When He indwells as the spirit of faith He will also become the spirit of praise.

But again, this should comfort us in trial; our Brother is bearing all that we bear and if He can stand it, surely we can. His Father would not allow His own beloved Son to have a needless pain and therefore we may be sure that there is a "need be" for all we are called to bear. If Christ is carrying the other end of the yoke, we may know it is right and that we shall not sink under the load. Let us then rejoice that we are partakers of the sufferings of Christ that "when His glory shall be revealed we shall be glad also with exceeding joy" (See 1 Peter 4:13).

Let this comfort us amid imperfect experiences and realizations of victory. "We see not yet all things put under Him." How true this is to us all! How many things there are that seem to be stronger than we are; but blessed be His name! They are all in subjection under Him and we see Jesus crowned above them all, and Jesus is our Head, our representative, our other self, and where He is we shall surely be. Therefore when we fail to see anything that God has promised and that we have claimed in our experience, let us look up and see it realized in Him and claim it in Him for ourselves.

Our side is only half the circle—the heaven side is already complete; and the rainbow of which we see not the upper half shall one day be all around the throne and take in the other hemisphere of our now unfinished life. By faith, then, let us enter into all our inheritance. Let us lift up our eyes to the north and to the south, to the east and to the west, and hear Him say, "All the land that you see will I give them."

Let us remember that the circle is complete, that the inheritance is unlimited, and that all things are put under His feet. Have we counted this true without abatement, or have we discounted it and lost its fullness? Shall we not henceforth "Crown Him Lord of all," and put all things under His feet, and then, keeping step with Him, put our feet on the difficulties and adversaries that we have feared so long, and go out henceforth in the chariot of His Ascension, to sing as we ascend, "But thanks be to God, who always leads us in triumphal procession in Christ and through us spreads everywhere the fragrance of the knowledge of him" (2 Corinthians 2:14).

Other Books by A.B. Simpson

Christ in the Tabernacle
Christ in You
Christ of the Forty Days
The Cross of Christ
Danger Lines in the Deeper Life
Days of Heaven on Earth
Divine Emblems
The Fourfould Gospel
Gentle Love of the Holy Spirit
The Gospel of Healing
The Holy Spirit
In Step with the Spirit
Land of Promise
Larger Christian Life
Life of Prayer
Lord for the Body
Loving As Jesus Loves
Missionary Messages
The Names of Jesus
Portraits of the Spirit-filled Personality
Practical Christianity
Seeing the Invisible
Self Life and the Christ Life
Serving the King
The Spirit-filled Church in Action
The Supernatural
When God Steps In
When the Comforter Came
Wholly Sanctified
Word Made Flesh